BE A

HOW TO START A **BAKERY**

BUSINESS FROM SCRATCH

BAKERY FOOD TRUCK, BAKERY STOREFRONT, OR FROM YOUR OWN KITCHEN

BUSINESS PLAN ADVICE, LLC FORMATION & MORE!

BY

Michelle McManus

CSB Academy
Publishing Co

CSB Academy Publishing Co.

Cover Design

By

Stephanie Martin

First Edition

Contents

ACKNOWLEDGMENTS

I want to thank my partner, first and foremost, for being so unendingly patient, especially in the early years. Building a business was so much harder than I thought – I had no idea how taxes, finances, financing, and more worked. Your love, support, and help throughout this time was the only reason I was able to truly succeed and be where I am, where we are, now.

My family was also an amazing source of inspiration and help. From my uncle Joe who told me that my rosemary shortbread tasted like earth and sadness (yikes) to my sister, Mae, who probably ate 100 different flavors of cupcakes over the course of six months and never once complained. Even when I made that Macha and lemon monstrosity that we never have to talk about again.

My friends who always came to events at my bakery and would never let me give them free cookies and cupcakes. Your support, love, and dedication to not just any local business, but my local business, really gave me the drive and motivation to keep going. I'm not sure if I would have had the will to keep pushing so hard if you hadn't been so wonderful to me.

Finally, I would like to give my never-ending thanks to my community. Your love and support meant that my dream could become a reality, and without you, I would have nothing. Thank you to everyone that supports local, small businesses and every single customer who has offered me a smile in exchange for a muffin, cupcake, or cookie.

INTRODUCTION

So you want to start your own bakery. Congratulations! This is a huge step. Even just sitting down to read this book is a monumental step towards completely changing your life. After all, that's the goal, right? When we start a new job, a business venture, or any other major happening, we are trying to change our life.

I'm here to help! I'm Michelle McManus, and I've had my own bakery business for over 15 years. I started baking much earlier than that, though, just out of my own kitchen. I had (and still have!) a passion and love for baking, experimentation, and creating something beautiful and delicious. I'm guessing we have that in common if you're reading this now.

I was baking out of my kitchen for myself when my obsession with new recipes far outweighed my ability to actually consume them. I started bringing my cookies, cakes, and cupcakes into work, where I was working in middle management in an unfulfilling job. People loved them.

I'll never forget my first "real" order. A coworker had a daughter getting married on a budget, and she wanted some cupcakes and cookies instead of a wedding cake. Of course, I said yes. I hadn't ever baked for an event before unless you counted the annual company-wide meetings, but I stayed up two days straight to get everything done in time.

The wedding was a total disaster, but someone from that wedding contacted me the next week for their son's 8th birthday party.

Thus, my home baking business was born.

It took a while to quit my unfulfilling job and even

longer to navigate the landscape of opening up a storefront, managing customers and employees, and actually turning a profit. My doors to my storefront have been open for over 15 years as of a few months ago, and we have established ourselves as a community staple. My niece and her husband do most of the day-to-day running of the business anymore, which is why I have the time and desire to write this.

Why should you care? Well, there's a point to telling you all about my life, I swear. It's so you understand that yes, I do know what I'm talking about. I went into my bakery business almost completely blind, but I had minored in business in college, and I had a ton of passion. I wanted my bakery to succeed not just for myself but to show others that you can achieve your dreams. I wanted out of my boring 9-5, and most of all, I wanted to be my own boss. I don't answer to anyone but myself. There are no boring meetings where I want to fall asleep, no email chains I need to keep up with, and I haven't sent the words "as per my last email" in years.

I've been where you have been, excited and wanting a different life, and I'm here to tell you it's completely possible. I'd love to help you achieve your dreams.

In this book, you're going to learn about the essentials not just of creating a business but a bakery. That could include finding and working out of a commercial kitchen or learning about cottage laws in your own state so you can cook in your kitchen. I'll help you understand what LLC means and how to establish yourself as one, and what you need to do in order to get your taxes above board, so you never have to worry about the IRS breathing down your neck. (Funnily enough, they take their money seriously... weird, I know)

I'm also going to help teach you how to build a business plan and secure additional funding if you don't have the upfront startup costs for your business sitting in a savings account.

We'll talk names, branding, and marketing, the biggest things you can do properly that will directly impact your success beyond having delicious products that people want to eat. After all, if your marketing is awful, no one will know you exist – and if your name is obscure, silly, or even offensive, people might not even want to give you a try.

I'm also going to help you figure out pricing, how to cut

your costs so you can actually make money, and how to know when you need to expand and hire more people – plus how to figure that price out in your budget, so you continue to make money while onboarding new staff.

Finally, I'll touch on how to sustainably grow your business so that you continue to thrive. Most people think all growth is good, but that isn't true at all – you want to be able to scale up properly. Think of it like a house of cards... if you build up too quickly, it will all come crashing down on you!

WHAT I'M NOT GOING TO TEACH YOU

I'm here to help with everything business. That's what I'm good at, that's what I've done for years, and really... it's something I love. I absolutely love seeing entrepreneurs get their ideas off the ground and become really successful.

What I'm not here to help with is the baking side. In this book, you won't find my secret gingerbread cookie recipe or how I get the perfect crumb on my best-selling cake, and I'm certainly not going to share the secret ingredient to my chai spiced sugar cookies. This is not a personal recipe book.

If you're looking for the recipes to sell, I suggest working in the kitchen yourself and figuring out what tastes good, what works and learning the foundations of baking. I even have a section to help you learn to develop your own recipes if you're struggling with how to get started. If you have great recipes and you're ready to start, this is the book for you.

FAST BAKERY STATISTICS

Spoiler alert: people love baked goods.

According to the American Bakers Association, bakery products make up over 2% of the gross domestic product of the US. The baking industry generates about $30 billion annually, with approximately 3,000 commercial bakeries all over the country.

The good news for us is that well over half of the bakeries are considered small. Sixty-five percent of them, in fact, have less than 10 employees. Forty-four percent have between one and four, and the majority of small retailers have just one single facility they bake out of.

Something to consider is that bread is the leader of the baking industry – no real surprise, since almost everyone eats bread, sandwiches, and more. Thirty-two percent of the market is bread, with 19% being rolls, 15% cakes, and pie coming in at just 2%. No love for pies, folks?!

In the coming decade, the bakery industry is expected to continue to grow by at least 1% annually. More disposable income and greater access to bakeries and baked goods will continue to drive the market. This is great news for someone who is considering opening their own bakery. That means even in a market with competition, there may be room for you.

In addition, with the huge changes happening in the world right now, many consumers are changing their focus and moving away from larger companies, looking instead to local and small businesses. This creates a big opportunity for someone just like you, hoping to make it in your own community as a small business.

How to Use This Book

I have taken the time to write what I think will be the most helpful for you as you approach this new journey. In the first chapter, we talk about the types of bakeries and what might work for you, what a cottage food law is and if it will apply to you, and all about working in a commercial kitchen.

Next, I go into the pros and cons of opening a physical storefront to sell your goods. It's not as black and white as you might think, and it is a huge decision, so be sure you give it the proper thought and weight it deserves. It's not always better to open an actual location.

Finally, we get into the next two chapters – or, as I referred to them when writing them, the boring but totally necessary sections. The first will go into writing a business plan, finding a name, and legally registering your business as an LLC (probably. You'll see). The second will walk you through business taxes, getting official with the IRS, managing your business insurance, and how to handle funding. Do you want a loan? Do you want an investor? We'll touch on it.

Then, the fun stuff comes. Your branding and target market is a huge part of your business, and it's important to treat them as such. This is also enjoyable to think about and will make your business feel more of a reality and less of a pipe dream.

Once you get that sorted, it's time to talk online. I'll go over if you need a website (you do) if you need social media pages (you totally do), and how to set those up.

Then, we'll go over marketing. It sounds intimidating to some, but I promise marketing your business doesn't have to be hard. It's a few clicks, some thoughtful words, and you have a full marketing plan.

Food safety is next, and it's vital you take it seriously. Some of you reading might have experience in a professional kitchen, and you understand how important cross-contamination is, but if you don't, this section is of vital importance. I also offer advice on how to handle cleaning your kitchen, commercial, or home.

Hiring is next on our list, and I go into creating an employee handbook, setting expectations, and more. At some point, you're going to have to hire someone, so it's important you start thinking about it now, even if right now it's a far-off thought.

Pricing and saving money are next, and we're almost to the end. Your pricing is obviously important, and you want to make sure you're making money while also offering value to your customers. You should never cut your margins so close that you have no emergency fund or you can't pay your bills. I have included a few of my personal favorite money-saving tips that I picked up while building my business and other things I have pulled from businesses while on this journey.

In the second to last chapter, I talk about your growth and continuing to succeed. After all, you probably don't just want to be kind of successful; you want to maximize every single aspect to make the most money and keep your customers happy! I'm not saying you need to, should, or can turn into the next Starbucks or Tim Hortons, but you can keep growing, expanding, and doing good.

Finally, I end with what every good book ends up – my final thoughts, a few helpful hints, and moving forward, what you should keep in mind.

I highly recommend on your first read-through of this book to read it cover to cover, even if some sections don't apply to you right at this moment, and have a notebook with you. You can also keep notes on your phone, on a tablet, or on a computer.

There are a few sections, like in the business plan section, where I may pose some questions for you to answer. In other sections, I offer helpful hints, tips, and advice I have used myself. Highlight these sections in the book; if you want to come back to them, write down anything that jumps out at you, and if you have inspiration or an idea while you are reading, be sure to write it down. This notebook will be sort of a guide for you going forward, with goals, plans, and more. Keep it close, and help it guide you.

There is no real wrong way to follow your dreams and open your own business. As long as you're smart, you're considerate, and you're realistic, you can make this happen.

Are you ready to start your journey?

WHAT TYPE OF BAKERY AND LEGALITIES INVOLVED WITH THEM

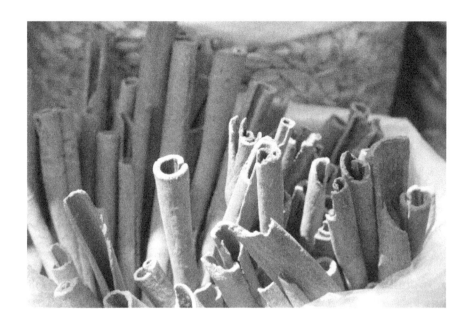

If you just woke up this morning and thought, I'm going to start a bakery, picked up this book, and decided to hit the ground running, that's awesome! But... for most of us, that's not how it happens.

Thinking about starting a bakery is like a small nagging feeling in the back of your mind that you could do something more with what you have. It starts small, a comment by a neighbor or friend that your goods are as good or better than what they buy at the store. A joke that "you could sell these" from a coworker.

It blossoms like a tiny seed. But for many, it just says that way, a little seed in the back of your mind as a what-if. And for most of us, that is because the business side is overwhelming. Don't close this book just because the first chapter has the word "legalities' in it. I promise this isn't scary, and you can tackle this project! Let's talk about the type of bakery you want to start first and how to make that happen.

TYPES OF BAKERIES

"There are different types of bakeries?!" You might be asking me. Yes, there are – and I'm going to help you go through these types to figure out what is best for your burgeoning business.

The truth is, the world has changed a lot, not just in the last forty or fifty years, but in the last ten to fifteen. When I first started my baking journey, I couldn't imagine a bakery solely relying on online sales and their website, but there are numerous bakeries all over the US doing exactly that... and they're very successful!

The rules of running and building a business have changed, and keeping up with the times is incredibly important in being successful in today's world.

TRADITIONAL STYLE IN-PERSON BAKERY

This is probably the bakery type that everyone thinks of when you tell them, "I want to start a bakery!". This bakery probably has a seating area, serves coffee and tea along with cold drinks, and may have other menu items like breakfasts or lunch, maybe served on or with some baked goods from your menu, like house-made bread.

The upsides to this traditional style are that it's exactly what people think about when they think about opening a bakery. If you've always dreamed of serving someone a cup of coffee, a muffin from your own recipe, and watching them settle into a café table or booth while they read and enjoy your goods, this is for you.

The downsides for this are that, by far, this takes the most capital. You need to secure a location, at least a small number of staff (one person cannot run an entire in-person bakery by themselves, not sustainably at least), do lots of market research... it's a lot. You are also tied to that location. If you get in, set everything up, and realize that there are major issues with the location like parking, foot traffic, and more, well, you're stuck – and that's not a bummer, but a huge financial concern.

20 years ago, if you wanted to start a bakery, this was the only choice. Now, most experts recommend not starting this way and instead going with one of our following options to build a customer base and work out all the 'quirks' of owning and running a business before putting down roots.

SPECIALIZED BAKERIES

Specialized bakeries are very popular in larger cities but tend to be rarer in a smaller community. These bakeries generally only have a few things for sale; it's things they do very, very well. This could be catering to an allergen, like a gluten-free bakery, or somewhere that makes the best scones, cookies, pies, scones, croissants... you get the idea.

There are a few ways you can run a bakery like this. Some choose a traditional style, with a sit-down café. Others prefer to go with a less traditional method, operating out of a rented commercial kitchen or even from your own home kitchen. Delivery methods for a less than traditional style can be take out only, delivery online, or even an online method.

CATERING-ONLY BAKERIES

Wedding planners, event management companies, and even banquet centers often need to work with a baker in order to help with their events, from cookie tables to wedding cakes, fresh bread for events... that sort of thing. Most of this business is gained from referrals and long-term contracts, but once you secure these things, it can be a very stable and even lucrative business.

The downside is that it can be hard to break into this business and niche. A lot of networking needs to be done, and each event isn't just evaluated on the success of what you make, but who else sees it. You never know who is going to be there and what next 'gig' they could offer you.

These bakeries can be run from a commercial kitchen – borrowed, rented, or owned – or a home kitchen. However, you're going to need a pretty sizable home kitchen to manage the scale of most catering orders.

The majority of takeaway-only bakeries work out of a commercial kitchen and serve local retail stores or coffee shops. Some takeaway-only bakeries also have their own small retail space. While there isn't enough room for tables, chairs, or lingering, customers can walk up to the counter and purchase your baked goods, along with perhaps a coffee or tea to go.

This is a nice balance between a less structured business and a traditional bakery because you can still have a storefront location – but it's smaller and easier to manage and maintain. The downsides still apply, however, with having to do lots of market research on the area you plan to open in. You still run the risk of tying yourself to a less than ideal location. And, you still need lots of capital to find a location and get it running.

FOOD TRUCK BAKERY

This has grown in popularity over recent years. Obviously, you wouldn't really be baking your goods in a food truck – there simply isn't enough room. Instead, your food truck would bring baked goods to various locations, like festivals, office events, even weddings.

Food trucks are chic and fun, but there are obvious downsides, too. Buying your own truck is a fairly expensive investment upfront, and then you need to modify both the interior and the exterior to look the way you want for your brand. While you don't have overhead costs like rent, you do need somewhere to store it (check with your neighborhood HOA, because food trucks are often not permitted in local areas), as well as pay for gas and regular maintenance.

You also need to secure a kitchen to cook out of. Depending on food laws, you may be able to bake from your own kitchen. Otherwise, you'll need a commercial kitchen at least part-time to prepare and package all your goods.

ONLINE-ONLY BAKERY

The latest in the bakery business is an online-only business. This format wouldn't have been available even a few years ago, but as consumers spend more time and money online, they are far more open to buying baked goods in less than traditional ways.

The biggest benefit of the online-only model is that it has the smallest startup costs. Depending on the laws in your area, you may be able to work out of your own kitchen. At the most, you need to rent a commercial kitchen to work out of, as no customers will ever be entering your work space.

You can ship or deliver your goods, depending on the proximity of your customers. The type and scope of your goods will only be limited to what you can produce.

Most of the businesses are smaller scale, though not always. The biggest way you reach your customers is through online marketing, word of mouth, and large orders.

DECIDING WHAT MODEL IS RIGHT FOR YOU

For many, it's difficult to figure out the right business model for your chosen business. In my personal experience, it's best to start with research.

Do some Googling, drive around the area you live in or love, and look at competitors in your area. Who is selling products that you also want to sell?

I recommend doing this in a methodical and measured way. Make a list of all the bakeries in the area or even coffee shops that sell baked goods. Write down their biggest offerings or what they sell the most. While you're making these lists, think about what you want to sell.

Don't worry – I'm going to go more in-depth with market research later, but doing some initial research will help you figure this part out.

By this point, you should at least have an idea of the type of goods you want to sell. As I mentioned before, I'm not here to tell you what to sell or how to bake it. That's on you and what you can make well. However, I will tell you to use some logic and deduction. If there are 5 bakeries within a 5-mile area selling just croissants, or bagels, or wedding cakes, that might not be the market you want to try and break into. There may simply be too much competition, even if your goods are delicious.

Look for where the hole in the market is. Do no bakeries serve pie, for example? What about modern or unique flavors of cookies or cakes? What do you think you can do well that the area doesn't have?

While you're doing your research, I highly suggest you go into any local physical locations and taste test their goods. Check out the atmosphere, and make notes about what you like and don't like, especially if you're going to be opening a physical location. Is there no good Wi-Fi? Nowhere comfortable to sit and meet? No larger gathering areas for book clubs or crochet groups?

Take notes on the food, too. What is the price of their goods, and do you feel the quality and taste are worth that price tag? Feel free to ask the owner about their business model or practices, but be aware that I personally have not had a good experience in this regard. Naturally, you're going to be looked at as potential competition, and they may not be willing to share information with you. If you want to maintain a good relationship with that location, I don't recommend it.

When you're looking at online businesses, either locally or nationally, do the same thing. Check out their website, and even order some things from each site. You're going to specifically look for bakery businesses that are both successful (or appear that way) and that will cater to the baked goods or market you're thinking about making and targeting. If you're not sure what that means yet, keep reading because I have a detailed section soon on finding your target market.

When you order, pay attention not just to the quality of the goods you're buying but their packaging and shipping practices. How well are the boxes packaged? Did your goods arrive without getting damaged or squished? What sort of custom or unique designs do they have? What do you like and dislike about their website, packaging, and products?

Consider the whole order process, from start to finish, to see where you can improve for your own business. You're looking for an easy, streamlined ordering process, quick delivery, and high-quality packaging and goods.

The hardest thing is when you're considering a catering bakery. You really can't order just one or two of those items; you often need to order a large selection. They really don't make 'just a few' cookies, cakes, or scones in these situations. The only way you're going to be able to test their goods or services is by going to an event that they are catering to. You can research prices, though, and what goods they offer, as well as ask around or check out reviews to see what people like or dislike about their services.

COTTAGE FOODS LAWS

"What does cottage food laws mean, and does it apply to me?"

Great question!

Depending on your state, the laws regarding selling products made in your own home for consumption are going to vary. Each state has a different legal requirement, and some don't acknowledge cottage food laws at all, meaning if you want to start a bakery business, you must go through a commercial kitchen.

In California, for example, cottage food laws are very specific. There is a list of 35 food items or types that fall under the approved food products. These foods may be made in your own kitchen and sold as long as you follow a set of regulations. This includes fruit pies, baked goods without meat, cream, or custard filling, confections like fudge and chocolate-covered candies or nuts, frosting, and icing that does not contain cream cheese, eggs, or cream, and even waffles or donuts. The goal for these "approved foods" is that they have a lower chance of carrying food-borne illnesses.

In California, there is also an income limit. With every state, this can be different – in CA, it's $50,000 in gross annual sales within a single calendar year. Once a home bakery makes more than that $50,000, they must move their production to a commercial kitchen.

California also requires bakers to complete a food handling course and obtain a food safety and sanitation certificate. This is fairly standard across the board, though, honestly? It's good practice even if you're not required to have it.

The biggest issue for California home bakers is that the food must be sold in person. This could be wholesale from a local restaurant or café, from your own, or at a farmers' market. However, the goods cannot be shipped to a customer, so an online-only business model where goods are shipped is not allowed.

Most states also require certain labeling to be present. This could be as simple as requiring all ingredients to be listed or as intense as noting on the label in a specific font size or style that it is a good made in a home kitchen.

You need to do research on what your own state allows before you sell from your home. It's absolutely imperative that you follow the law. If you choose to go your own route and ignore your local state laws, you could end up with fines that far exceed any income you had from your business.

If you're ever concerned about what goods fall under your own state's cottage laws or what certifications you need, you can reach out to your states' Department of Agriculture, which handles these regulations. The more specific you are with your questions, the better answers you're going to get. If you know of a local bakery that also works from their own home kitchen, you may be able to reach out to them and ask about their own experience with your state's cottage food laws.

COMMERCIAL KITCHENS: DO I NEED ONE?

If you can't work out of your home kitchen due to the type of food you're making, the sales you're doing, or if your kitchen is simply too small, you're going to need a commercial kitchen instead.

The biggest benefit to renting a commercial kitchen is it has an official license, and the government has handled all the details of certifying the kitchen for safety and sanitation. There are a lot fewer 'legal' hoops to jump through before you're able to start baking, and you don't have to deal with the hassle of it all.

There are a few types of kitchens you may run into while you're looking into this process.

A shared kitchen is a commercial kitchen that is essentially what it sounds like, a shared space. You aren't the only one using it. Often these have a 'sign up' time, and you register for the hours you want to use the kitchen. Perhaps you need a few hours a few times a week, or just once a week to produce. You're going to sign up for that time slot, and you're only allowed to be there during that time.

Often, many different small businesses or bakeries are using this space, too. Sometimes small businesses or restaurants will rent out their kitchen when they are closed, or a large church may rent their commercial kitchen out when they aren't using it. Even schools or hotels may offer this, so if using a shared space appeals to you, be sure to look – and ask! – around to see what your options are.

A commissary is designed for businesses like yours. They are licensed and all ready to use. Often food trucks or smaller bakeries rent these spaces. They are outfitted and ready to go, and all you need to do is step in and start working. You can store, cook, and even sometimes package in these spaces. You still need to work within the confines of the kitchen's hours and regulations, but you have a little more freedom than a shared space.

Finally, a private kitchen is the most expensive option. You have full and total control over the space and access anytime you need it, but in a private kitchen, you have full access to everything, and you can often store things for long periods of time.

I NEED A PHYSICAL LOCATION: HOW DO I FIND ONE?

Don't fret! If you want a traditional, café style bakery, or even a takeout-only location, I have you covered in the next chapter! Keep reading, and you'll learn all about the complexities of finding the perfect location for you. Which, trust me, is a lot harder than it sounds.

Ask Lots of Questions

Before you enter into a contract with a rental kitchen, be sure to ask a ton of questions and then ask some more. This is even more complicated than renting an apartment because the rules are often ill-defined.

Be sure you understand everything that is and isn't included with the kitchen rental. Sometimes you'll get lucky, and there will be a big industrial mixer or plenty of equipment ready for you to go, and it will come with the space. More often, though, you're going to need to supply much of your own equipment.

Ask what is permitted and what isn't. Most commercial kitchens completely ban anything that is for consumer use, so your home mixer or blender may not be allowed to make the journey to the commercial kitchen. You may have to purchase or rent equipment that is specifically for bakeries or food businesses, costing you a lot more. Ask for a written listen of what you can't bring in, and always keep a copy.

Even if a mixer is on the property, it may not always be

available. If you will be sharing the space with another business, be sure to inquire about availability. Is using the equipment in your contract? Are you promised these items, or is it more of a first-come, first-served sort of situation? What happens in the event of damage to these items or regular maintenance – if you're relying on this equipment to be there and something happens to it, are they required to provide alternative solutions?

In general, most commercial kitchens will have, at minimum, an oven, a freezer, a fridge, and a grill. Since we're talking about starting a bakery, not a food truck, you should probably try to find a space that has multiple ovens or even a professional-grade convection oven for faster cooking.

Other things, like pots, pans, and trays, may or may not be included. Again, be sure to get a list of what is included in your rental and where all of it is stored. Some commercial kitchens don't care at all and have a huge stock of equipment and tools you can use. Others won't even offer you a spatula, and you need to provide all of your tools and equipment.

Before you sign anything, compare the list of tools they

offer to the things you know you need for your business. Little unexpected expenses add up quickly, so you need to know you can cover everything and not be hit with a surprise price tag down the line.

Finally, ask about insurance and other liabilities. Do they require you to carry your own business insurance into that kitchen, and if so, how much do you need to be insured for? Some rentals will allow you to fall under their own insurance, so you only need a minimum. Others may require you to have $1 million or more of insurance in case of accidents before you can even turn on the stove.

How Do I Even Find a Commercial Kitchen?!

Great question. If you need to find a commercial kitchen for rent, ask around. Like many industries, the culinary world is very tight-knit. Everyone knows someone who knows someone and asking a friend in the foodservice industry is absolutely your best bet. If they don't know of something right off the top of their head, there's a good chance they can ask around and find you something or score you a deal.

If that fails, reach out to local groups or marketplaces.

Your area's local subreddit or Facebook groups might be an invaluable resource, and you could find someone who has exactly what you need.

Finally, there are some online platforms that may help. Places like The Kitchen Door and Peerspace are sites that help connect people like you with commercial space for rent. I've helped startups using The Kitchen Door and have had some great results. Do your research and read reviews before you sign a contract with a complete stranger!

Note: Don't go sign a contract tomorrow! Slow down, finish this book, and weigh your options before diving in headfirst. A good plan involves multiple steps, so be patient and take your time. You won't find success from running in half-blind, I'm sorry to say.

THE ADVANTAGES OF WORKING FROM YOUR OWN KITCHEN

If cottage laws aren't an issue and you can work out of your own kitchen for a while, there are a lot of benefits.

For one, you are basically working from home. Unless

you're leaving your house to get ingredients or buy supplies, you don't have to go anywhere to start your workday. You can get up at 4 am to start baking or go to sleep at 4 am, because it's your kitchen and your rules.

You also know exactly where everything is, and chances are, you're very comfortable in your home kitchen. After all, this is where your business really started, from knowing how the oven works (fun fact: my own home oven runs 10 degrees cooler than it should. Exactly ten, according to my in-oven thermometer) to knowing where all your supplies are, knowing just what setting to use to melt butter, and even just how cold your freezer gets.

Because you're comfortable in this setting, you may be more likely to work faster and produce better final products. It's just one of those facts of life.

You can also dress how you want. Want to wear pajama pants and a tank top to make a batch of cookies? You do you. There's no one else sharing the space and no risk of running into anyone in your own kitchen. The comfort level is through the roof.

My favorite thing about working in my own home

kitchen was being able to pop into my spare bedroom (also known as our office) if I needed anything. I could walk the dog when he needed walked, I could have my laptop on and listen to music or watch a show while I baked and cleaned up. I was comfortable.

THE DISADVANTAGES OF WORKING FROM YOUR OWN KITCHEN

Just as there are upsides, there are downsides, too. Being comfortable in a space is great, but if you're too comfortable, it can be easy to 'forget' you're there for a job, not just baking for pleasure. Maybe you put off making a batch of cookies because you know it won't take long and end up running against deadlines or watching just one more episode of your favorite show instead of getting started. I'm not here to judge you because it has happened to us all at some point.

There are a lot of distractions at home. If you have kids, a spouse, or pets, you might end up finding out that you're spending as much time dealing with them as you are taking care of your business needs, no matter how much you're personally dedicated or how good your intentions are.

Frankly, it's hard to work from home. It's a lot. If you don't have a real dedication and drive, it's all too easy to just... not.

Space is also a big issue for many folks baking from home. If your kitchen is the size of a postage stamp and you have no storage, you may struggle with being able to bake in bulk. When you do cookies for a friend, you may be making a dozen or two. If you're baking for many people and many orders, you may be making several dozen cookies in different flavors. Can your kitchen handle this? Can your oven handle this?

Do you have space to pack as well? After all, you're not just baking at home – you're going to be packaging your goods for sale, either online sales or in-person sales. You're going to need room for all of that. A dining room is great for that, but you won't be using that space for dining for a long time.

Finally, the biggest downside in my opinion to working at home is the equipment. I didn't realize this was a downside until I transitioned into a commercial kitchen, but wow, does professional equipment make a difference. I could bake well and consistently in my home kitchen, but I baked fantastically in a commercial kitchen, with a professional mixer, convection oven, etc.

At home, you're limited to home use equipment. Even the biggest home kitchens probably don't have space for an industrial mixer, obviously. You can only make so much because of the equipment you have access to. Even rotating your oven or running your mixer constantly, at some point, you may simply max the number of things you can make.

THE ADVANTAGES OF WORKING FROM A COMMERCIAL KITCHEN

Many people simply cannot handle working from home. Their brain doesn't switch to 'work mode' until they get to work. When you have a commercial kitchen to work from, as soon as you walk through the door, you're in work mode and focused on work. There are no distractions, no kids running, to dogs needing attention... it's just work.

This also helps you disconnect from the business. When you're working out of your own home, it can be easy to fall into the trap where you do just a bit more, and it takes over every waking moment. By working out of a specified space, when you come home, you can really 'be home' and unwind. For some, this isn't an issue, but if you are a type A or a workaholic, you know exactly what I'm talking about.

Depending on the space you have, you should have access to commercial-grade equipment – whether you have to buy and bring it with you or it comes with your space. As I mentioned before, commercial-grade equipment is a huge step up from using equipment in your home, and this can really make a big difference in the quality you're able to produce and the amount you produce. I have a Kitchen Aid mixer at home, don't get me wrong, but it can't touch a professional mixer.

You don't have to worry about cottage food laws because you're working from a professional space. This is a really big deal, especially if you live in a state that is very strict. Sometimes, the only way you can get your bakery off the ground is a commercial kitchen.

Finally... you usually have space. Even in a small commercial kitchen, there is counter space, a packaging area (if there's not, you picked the wrong kitchen!), and room to breathe. If you're used to working out of a small home kitchen, this is going to be a breath of fresh air, truly.

THE DISADVANTAGES OF WORKING FROM A COMMERCIAL KITCHEN

Without a doubt, the biggest disadvantage of working from a commercial kitchen is the price. You're paying for the space, and depending on where you're located, you're probably spending a decent bit. This overhead can be very hard for a new business or bakery to manage, and an expensive commercial kitchen can end a business before it has even begun. Dark? Sure, but true.

It can also be overwhelming to start. If you already have a kitchen ready to go, you may not know where everything is, how to find it, and more. In addition, you don't necessarily know how all the equipment works. This can be overwhelming and seriously put a damper on the amount of work you can get done once you get into your space. Eventually, it will balance out, but the adjustment period is rough.

You also have to leave your house to get there. Sounds obvious? I know – but if you live in an area with very bad weather, or you live very far from your commercial kitchen, it can be difficult to make it every workday. You can't really call out sick… you're the boss! It's on you to be there each and every day you have decided and get things done, no matter how far the drive is or how the weather is. The only person it negatively impacts if you miss it is you.

HOW DO I DECIDE WHAT'S RIGHT FOR ME?

I can't tell you the right choice, I'm sorry to say. I don't know the size of your home kitchen, the scope of work you want to make, or your own personality and quirks.

With nearly every small business, I recommend starting as small as possible and scaling up. If you can launch your business from your home kitchen, even for six months, to build a clientele up and start making money before transitioning into another option, I highly recommend it. Having that experience and time to work out any kinks and really feel your way through how running a bakery business works before you have to invest so much money into it really makes sense and can save you a ton of cash in the long run.

For others, due to restrictive cottage laws, family issues, small home kitchens, and more, it simply might not be possible, and you need to start in a commercial environment. That's totally okay, too, but keep in mind that the best way to start is to start small, so don't be afraid to only rent a space a few hours a week at first to get your feet wet and figure it all out.

A PHYSICAL STOREFRONT: PROS AND CONS

So you want a physical storefront. Maybe you've decided to branch out from your home kitchen, cottage laws require you to work out of a commercial kitchen anyway, or you're really determined to get that classic bakery feel. Whatever your reasons, if you need a physical location customers can go into to either just pick up goods for takeout or sit down and enjoy their morning, you're going to need to do some research.

Just getting the first location that looks good enough

isn't a good idea at all. There is a ton of research and decision-making that needs to go into this choice. I'm sorry to say if you thought you were moving into a location next week... well, let's just start from the top.

MAKE A LIST

I'm a big fan of lists, but my love of them doesn't have anything to do with the sheer practicality of this statement. Sit down with this book, a piece of paper, and a pencil.

Divide the page into two sections – things you need and things you would like to have but don't particularly need.

A commercial kitchen? A need. An oven large enough to handle your volume? Probably a need, too. Plenty of fridge space for butter, milk, and eggs? Certainly a need; you're going to go through a ton of the stuff. Storage space for flour, sugar, and other dry goods? Yep, a need too.

At first, this is going to seem easy, and let the ideas come to you. Ask yourself before you write it in the need or want category if it's really a need or just a want – or, if you can't live without it, making it a true need.

Then let's think about our other needs. Who is shopping at your store, buying your baked goods? Are you going to rely on commuters that travel from your smaller town to a local bigger one? Do you want a lot of foot traffic, so you need to be in a shopping district or a downtown area? Do you want to get that college kid crowd, meaning you need to be within walking distance of campus in a hot spot?

These things are important! You know your area, so be sure to consider the demographics of your area and who may be the most interested in buying your baked goods.

Not sure about your demographics? If you're in the US, and I'm presuming you are, the US Census Bureau lets you search by a range of variables, including zip code, county, and city, to find information on the area's income level, ages, and even ethnicities. You can also check out your county or state government's websites, which should have some additional information for you.

This is really helpful to use not only to know where to look but where not to look. If you're selling $5-$7/piece baked goods, you probably should not put your bakery in an area where the median household income is less than

$30,000, after all, or an area that does not draw an outside market. The households in the area simply can't afford what you're offering with enough regularity to build and maintain your business and expenses.

I'm going to talk more about market research in a later chapter, so stay tuned.

Depending on where you live, you're going to want to do research in several areas around you to see where your bakery will fit best. For some smaller towns, there may really only be one or two spots within a reasonable distance to your home or workplace to choose from. Just be sure you check out the demographic of the area and know who your customer is!

Consider the other businesses in your prospective area, too. Drive around, walk around, look at the surrounding businesses. Are you looking in an area that doesn't have a fresh bakery or an area that has 3 within a two-mile radius? If there are an overwhelming number of bakeries that could compete with your business, this may not be the best location for you.

Here's a question: are you going to purchase your commercial property for your bakery, or are you going to lease it from a management company?

When you purchase the property, it works just like purchasing a home. You buy the property, either outright with cash or with a loan, and you have control over the property itself. You can upgrade things as needed, change anything you dislike, and you potentially get tax breaks for mortgage expenses or interest paid on the loan.

You also have equity in the property, obviously. If it appreciates, you will gain money, and you own your own building. No worries about the property changing owners, unstable landlords, or anything else.

There are downsides, though. There is at least some upfront payment required, just like with buying a home. If you aren't well-financed, you may not have that upfront money. If you or your business don't have a strong track record of success, you may struggle with even qualifying for a loan at all.

Extensive insurance – more insurance than your business itself needs – will also be required. Usually, the owner of the building will carry liability insurance on the building itself. As the building owner, you're going to need to do this yourself.

You're also on the hook for any and all building maintenance. Many times, when you lease a building, at least some of this is covered within your lease. Instead, when you purchase your building and the land around it, it's yours. Lawn care, any basic upkeep, any additional upgrades... all you.

The benefits of leasing are, of course, you don't have to worry about this. You won't need to secure so much funding to start because you're only leasing. You'll need some money upfront, of course, but you won't need a down payment's amount.

If something happens to the property, it's often not ultimately up to you. Depending on the lease you sign, the landlord may take care of lawn care, extensive maintenance, and more. These are all things you don't have to stress about, and you can put your focus back into your business instead.

If the market turns, you don't have to worry about the depreciation of your building, too.

It's all up to you – I can't tell you which is right for your situation. I will say that purchasing a property is a much bigger commitment and comes with a lot more stress.

MEET WITH A REALTOR

Maybe you already know exactly the location, you've done your research, and you know there is a perfect location for rent or sale. But if you're like the rest of us, you're going to need some help to figure out where you belong.

Contact a real estate professional that handles commercial properties, not your Aunt Susan or Cousin George, who sells houses. These are two very different professionals. You should also try to find a realtor that works with businesses like you, looking for spaces. You don't want a realtor that works with landlords specifically because they're going to be looking out for more the interest of their clients (the landlords) rather than the businesses (you!).

Once you find a realtor you like, it's time to start looking at properties. You should be asking a lot of questions, whether you're buying or leasing your property, including:

What equipment in the kitchen is included? What, if anything, in the front is included?

What will the landlord allow you to change? Are minor remodels allowed? What about major ones?

Will the landlord cover any remodels to the building to bring it up to the modern-day? Will they supply any additional equipment? (Always worth asking!)

What else is included in the lease? Will the landlord be covering things like lawn care or signage? What about repairs? Make sure it's all spelled out clearly in the lease; leave nothing to question.

What was the business before it became available?

Is the location safe? This may be a question you need to do research on to answer, but find out what the realtor or landlord has to say about it, too. Was the building ever robbed?

Is the building equipped with everything you need to be successful, or will you have to supply major kitchen or front office equipment, like convection ovens or freezers?

What does the lease say about rising prices? Can they just hike up the price next year when you re-sign, or is there a clause in the lease about a certain percent increase each year?

Who owns the building? Is it a single person? A management company? A huge company that owns dozens and dozens of buildings? There are good and bad aspects to both sides – with a single owner, it can be messy or less than professional. With a large company, however, it can be difficult to get their attention or have issues addressed.

Does the lease have an "out" clause? This is basically when you can state that you can leave the space for specific reasons, like growing quickly and needing more room or issues with the business and operations.

Other things you need to consider when you view properties include:

Is there parking? Is it in a location that needs parking,

or is it in a downtown area that gets a lot of foot traffic? Personally, I specifically avoid shopping at places that have difficult parking because I hate tight, small parking lots. I know I'm not alone. Think about how your customers are going to get into your business.

Is it near a main road? If you're just off a highway or other busy road, you may have a better chance of attracting more customers. If customers have to go out of their way to get to you, they are less likely to stop by. Being on a morning commute or a daily route will increase your traffic.

Does your ideal customer live, work, or shop in this area? If you want to target folks who stop before work to get breakfast, a location near a major office park might be a great idea. If you want to target college kids in your college town, a spot that they can walk to from campus is ideal.

Do you understand the lease? I'm not trying to be rude – legalese is confusing even to lawyers sometimes, so before you ever sign anything, be sure to read it thoroughly and then ask an attorney to go over it. This sounds like an expensive step, but you're undertaking something major and expensive. Being sure you dot all your I's and cross all your t's, quite literally, is important.

How much is it going to cost to bring the building up to where you want it? This is an expense some new business owners don't consider or vastly underestimate. It's expensive to install furniture, buy equipment, and get a business off the ground. The bigger the space, the more potential maybe – but the more money you're going to invest, too. Be sure to do all of your homework on what you want to put into the building and how much it's all going to cost. Even "little" costs like paint or fixtures really add up. Consider contacting local contractors before signing to get quotes!

TYPES OF COMMERCIAL LEASES

There are 3 main types of leases you're going to come across: gross leases, net leases, and modified leases.

A gross lease is also sometimes called a full service lease, and it's the most encompassing lease type. Your rent to your management company or landlord covers everything else, like property taxes, maintenance, and even utilities.

This is a big plus for many tenants because you really don't have to stress about a lot, the landlord covers it all. In the summer, your electricity is going to go up because, duh, you're running the air conditioning more. You don't have to worry about that bill increase, though, because your landlord is covering the utilities.

This is also the most expensive type of lease, because you are asking your landlord to shoulder the majority of the costs of running your business. There are also sometimes escalation clauses written in these leases that allow landlords to increase rent or charge additional fees in case of something major happening, so be sure to read your lease very thoroughly.

A net lease is more common, and it is very adjustable and variable depending on the circumstances. Generally, the tenant pays a lot less to the landlord than in a gross lease situation, but in exchange, the tenant pays more of the operating costs, like common area maintenance, property tax, and even insurance.

A single net lease is where the tenant pays rent and a portion of the property taxes, along with utilities and other services. The landlord covers some of the building expenses.

A double net lease is the same as above, but the tenant pays part of the insurance as well. In exchange, the landlord pays for maintenance in the common areas. The tenant, however, is still expected to pay utilities and other services.

A triple net lease is where the tenant pays the rent, as well as taxes, insurance, and maintenance. Basically, the landlord is just there to collect the rent, and the tenant is responsible for all the other 'big' things. This is, by far, the most common type of lease you're going to find.

Finally, a modified gross or net lease is sort of a middle ground between the two others, if the name wasn't obvious enough. The amount of financial responsibility the tenant bears will vary depending on the landlord and negotiations, and each aspect needs to be agreed upon by both parties.

STAY ON BUDGET

The worst thing you can do as a new business is to deviate from a budget. You know your funding (and we'll talk about all this soon), and by the time you're ready to sign a lease, you should have an idea of what you can afford each month.

It's so important you stick to your budget! Otherwise, you're asking for trouble, heartache, and stress before you even open your doors.

If you have an in-person bakery, either takeout or a traditional style, the atmosphere is a huge deal. While we're talking about locations, I'm going to drop some helpful hints I've come across during my time running my own business that may assist you, too. As always, you should adapt any advice I have, or anyone else has, to your own concept and ideas.

Your customer's first impression of your bakery sets the tone for what is to come, without question. Think about your favorite restaurant or personal favorite bakery. What is their entrance like, and what do you like about it? Is there a restaurant or bakery you've visited that you absolutely hate the entrance of? Why? Is it poor lighting, awkward doors, or bad signage?

You should always make sure that your most eye-catching or visually appealing items are at eye level in your display case. This could be highly decorated cupcakes, cakes, the most intricate cookies... whatever you're selling that is most appealing to your customers.

More 'staple' items, or boring items, can be on lower shelves or even behind the counter, like bread. You want your big sellers to be front and center, taking up space.

Make sure everything about your bakery is welcoming and comforting. Plush couches are a café staple because people love them! Oversized, easy to hold mugs make for great conversational pieces, and customers often love the feel of a real, heavy mug versus a standard to-go cup.

Whatever you do, though, don't cram tables or chairs into a space. When customers come to a bakery they want privacy and space, so make sure everything is free of clutter (there's a fine line between decorations and clutter!) and spaced appropriately.

If you're going for an upscale cake shop type of vibe, neutral colors, and soft lighting are going to be your best bet. However, if you want a fun or vibrant atmosphere, don't shy away from bright colors or accent walls to give your bakery a fun personality.

I've seen businesses partner with local artists to do murals with great success. If that is the vibe you're going for, consider reaching out into the community to see who you can find! Not only will this give you a unique and fun vibe, but it also is a great way to increase and improve community engagement.

Ultimately, a good bakery is functional above all else. Your display cases need to work to show the best of your products, your layout needs to make sense for customers, and it all should be focused on selling your products above all else.

The idea of an 'open kitchen' has gained appeal in recent years, in a lot of different restaurants. However, I don't recommend this approach to most bakeries! The large equipment, speed racks, and other things aren't giving your customers an interesting or fun look into your bakery – they're just taking up visual space and creating distractions. Keep everything behind closed doors, if at all possible.

THE NITTY GRITTY OF STARTING YOUR BUSINESS, PART ONE

This is the part most potential business owners dread, but opening a bakery is more than just dreaming up recipes and baking in the mornings before you open. All of this chapter and the next, the nitty-gritty of starting your business, is very important! Let's tackle it one step at a time.

WRITING A BUSINESS PLAN

A business plan is actually very, very simple at the core

– don't get intimidated. Your business plan is a document that basically states the goals of your business, how you plan to reach those goals, and when you plan to reach them. It doesn't have to be long, complicated, or overly technical.

I will tell you that in our next chapter, I'm going to talk about securing funding for your business should you need it. If you're in the position to approach financial institutions or investors, you're going to need a professional business plan. However, even if you're not going to secure funding, a business plan is important.

It gives you a road map to follow, and goals to hit. It provides you, and your business, with much-needed structure and guidance. This is one of the many things that separates someone who is casually selling baked goods from a business owner.

There are two standard formats for business plans. One is the traditional, and one is the startup.

A traditional business plan is, well, traditional. They use a standard structure, include plenty of details, and are generally accepted everywhere.

A startup business plan is significantly leaner, usually only being a page or two at the very most. They go into very few details, and may only take an hour to write, edit, format, and print.

"I'll do the second one!" I'm sure you're saying. I get it! It's tempting to write the shorter one because, well, it's shorter, it's easier, and it's going to get you to your own personal 'finish line' sooner. However, I'm actually going to tell you right now, the longer and more traditional one is probably better.

If you're getting investors, you should absolutely choose the longer one. The more details you have (within reason, of course), the more likely people will believe and trust in you. A longer, more traditional business plan is just better overall.

There are a few standard steps to take when you're writing your business plan. Let's break it down piece by piece. I recommend opening a document on your PC or grabbing a notebook to jot down notes and answers to some of my questions (yes, there's a quiz. No, it's not graded!) to help keep your thoughts together.

At the start of any good business plan is an executive summary. This is essentially your introduction to the business. You're going to write what your company is, what you're going to be doing, and why you're going to be successful.

Let's work on some questions to get you thinking about your executive summary.

Who are you, and why do you want to start a bakery? What drives you to start a bakery?

What does this business mean to you? What would a successful business really mean to you? Personal, but a business is personal!

What type of products are you going to sell? Baked goods, obviously – after all, you're reading a book about starting your own bakery. But what type of baked goods? Are you a specialty bakery, selling just set products? Do you have a potential menu or ideal product line?

Where is your business going to be located? Will you be working out of your home kitchen, a commercial kitchen, or an actual physical location? You may not be sure exactly where you're going to be located yet, and that's okay, but if you have a plan to find a location, add that in!

Are you working by yourself, or will you be hiring employees? Do you already have employees, maybe a family member or friend that has committed to helping your business grow? This is where that goes, as well.

The executive summary is also where you're going to want to put your goals for the business. Your goals are... well, your goals. What do you want to accomplish with this business?

When you're writing out goals for your business, even outside of your business plan, I encourage you to use the SMART Goals System to help write realistic, manageable goals that you can hit. SMART stands for specific, measurable, achievable, relevant and time-bound. Each of your goals should hit these points.

For example, the goal "I want to be crazy-successful" is... probably true, honestly. Who doesn't want their business to take off and really make them successful? However, this goal is wildly vague. How do we define success? What does crazy successful even mean? By what time do we want to be crazily successful?

This is where the SMART system comes in.

Is my goal specific enough?

Your goals should be specific. What is it you want to happen? Where is your goal located, and what resources do you need to make that goal a success? What limits are there, and who is going to be involved in making this goal happen?

Why does this goal matter to me, or to my business? What is my driving force behind this goal?

If you can't answer these questions when you're setting business goals, it's time to go back to the drawing board and create a more specific goal.

Is my goal measurable?

What is the measure of success on your goal? You should always have a yardstick to success, essentially, and know when you hit your goals. "I want to be crazy successful" is great, but "crazy" is not a way to realistically measure success, so there is no measurable goal.

When you're writing down a goal, ask yourself, how long will it take me to get to my goal? How will I know when I've hit this goal? Do I have specific numbers? How many items or people does this goal involve to become a reality?

If you can't answer these questions, your goal is not measurable enough.

Is my goal achievable?

Yes, I'm going to use the same goal – "I want to be crazy successful." This isn't achievable because it's not defined enough. Your goal needs to be achievable and realistic. In my personal life, I have fitness goals, for example, but I'm never going to run in the Olympics, so that isn't on my goal list. It's simply not achievable.

When writing your goals down, ask yourself how you will accomplish that goal. Is it realistic when you consider both time and financial restraints placed on you currently? Is it within your current skill level and ability, or within your projected skill level and ability in a reasonable amount of time?

You're allowed to evaluate a goal and realize that it is not, in fact, achievable, at least at the moment. Your goals are always going to be changing and evolving as your business grows, and you need to set attainable, achievable goals now, and actually hit them. Setting huge, grand goals that are not actually achievable is truly just setting yourself up to be disappointed and discouraged, two things you do not need when starting a business.

Is my goal relevant?

This is a hard one, because it varies not just on the business type but your specific business goals and what you're selling. It's so easy to get caught up in an idea or concept and let that excitement take you away, but you need to make sure that your goals are relevant. Relevant to yourself, and your business, as well as your target market, and your own personal values, morals, and beliefs.

Your goals should always align with the core concept of your company – baking pies, gluten-free wedding cakes, birthday cookies... you know your business better than I do. But your goals should always be relevant to your concept.

Some questions you can ask while you are writing goals to ensure they are relevant include asking if this goal is even worth achieving? Will it better yourself and your business? Is it the right time within the company to work towards this goal, or is it pulling you further away from your core concept?

The most important one is this, though: does this goal align with the current and future needs of my business? If the answer is no, your goal is not relevant at this time.

Is my goal time-bound?

Finally, the last questions you need to ask yourself with your business goals are about time. If you're worked through the first part of the SMART system, by this point the answer is probably going to be yes, but you need to tick all the boxes just to be sure.

When will this goal be achieved, and who is achieving it? What progress can I make right at this moment to get me closer to this goal? What can I do in the next six weeks, six months, or year to make progress? Is this a goal that must be accomplished by a certain amount of time? Why or why not?

Open-ended goals are dangerous, because they may not give you the drive to actually achieve them. Setting goals with a timeline give purpose.

Always Use SMART

Once you start using the SMART system to create your goals, it's hard to go back. This is such an efficient way to create goals in any aspect of your life, and it really helps you break down your goals in manageable chunks.

If you have a goal that doesn't meet the SMART criteria, think about how you can piece it out into smaller bits that do. Bit by bit, you can work out that larger goal and make it happen.

THE COMPANY DESCRIPTION

The second section is going to be your description. A company description is basically just even more details about your business.

Is your business solving a problem? Perhaps your problem is that there are no quality bakeries in a specific neighborhood, or nowhere for residents to get a morning coffee and pastry on their way to work.

Detail your ideal customer and how you're helping solve their problems here. How do you fit into their lives?

Be sure to also list what will make your business successful over competing businesses. What gives you that competitive edge? Is it your experience? Your knowledge of your niche? What experts on your team have you recruited in order to get a step above? Maybe it's your location that will give you the edge?

YOUR MARKET ANALYSIS

Don't get scared! This isn't as complicated as it might sound. This is basically a look at your industry and your target market. I'm going to go more in-depth into doing research and mark analysis soon, so keep this section of your business plan in mind when you read that.

This section could include who you're selling to, and why you're targeting these folks. We talked about this a bit when we were discussing location, and I'll talk more in the branding section in our next chapter, but I want you to start thinking about who you're selling to. Is it college kids? Young professionals with allergies? Who is going to buy your product, and why?

You also might want to touch on trends in your market right now, and how you're reacting to them. There are always trends in businesses, but especially in the baking world. While the core of a bakery business hasn't really changed in the last 100 years (you're providing a service, which is baked goods), the way the business functions is so different. Between TV channels like Food Network and social media like TikTok and Instagram, pushing newer and better out each week, trends are always evolving.

You're also going to want to mention your competitors in this section. What research have you done on your direct competitors? What are they doing right? Are they successful, and is there room in the market for you? What are you going to do differently and better?

THE ORGANIZATION

If you are rolling solo with this, it's going to be a short section. However, if you're bringing in friends, family, or your spouse to help run the day-to-day business, they are going to go here. This section is going to include how your management system is structured (who is in charge of who?), and who will run the most important operations.

Laying out the structure of your organization is important not just for yourself, but for any employees you may have, and any investors interested in what you're offering. Clear, defined roles are what lead to a business's success. What roles are murky or chain of command is unclear; it can be very difficult.

If you have multiple employees, laying out the key employee's assets and what they bring to the table can be important, too. Some business plans even include the resumes of your key employees to highlight their experience – if you're searching for funding and you feel like you have an 'ace in the hole' in terms of a team, this is a good idea.

YOUR PRODUCTS

What are you selling? Yes, yes, baked goods, I know – but what type? What are your product lines? What all are you going to be offering, and what does your system look like?

This is more than just a paragraph about baking! This section should include types of products and why you're offering them, as well as any plans to do seasonal products, expand your line, and more.

THE MARKETING STRATEGY

I'm going to go into more details about marketing in a later chapter, but while you're building your business plan, you need to make sure that you talk about the type of marketing that you're going to run in order to drive business. There is no right or wrong way to handle marketing, and your customer base is going to really determine what type of marketing you use.

At the very least, this section is used to describe how you're going to get customers, and how you're going to keep them. Social media ads, Google Ads, local advertisements, and even setting up shop at a local farmers market could all be ways to get customers. Retaining customers could be through email campaigns to those who have already purchased, offering a punch card for loyal members, consistency, that sort of thing.

You also will want to use this section to talk about sales projections. How will sales happen? In person, online? Using what methods? What sales strategies do you have?

If you're writing this solely for the purpose of attracting investors or encouraging funding, this is where you're going to detail all your funding needs. And I do mean all. Banks, businesses, or private individuals always want to know exactly where their money is going, and you have an obligation to them to detail what you're going to do with their money and how you will spend it.

Be thorough. Talk about how much funding you're going to realistically need within the next 3-5 years, and what you're going to use it for. Are you paying salaries with this money? Buying equipment, like a mixer, an oven, etc.? Are you just paying overhead until your revenue stream increases, and your business can carry that weight itself?

You should specify if you're looking for debt or equity as well. Debt is exactly what you think it is, where you borrow a specific amount from an institution or person, and agree to repay in x number of years with y interest. Equity, however, is a share of the business. If someone offers you x money for a percentage of ownership in your business, that is an equity deal. They may be entitled to a voice in decision-making, a percent of income, and more.

This is also the section you'll put your projections on not just repaying any debt, but your "exit" plan. What if something happens and you need to step away from the business? This is where you'll talk about your plans, either selling the business as a whole or liquidating it. No one wants to think about this, but it's important to include an exit plan in case of emergencies.

YOUR FINANCIAL PROJECTIONS

This is sort of tied to your funding requests, in that if you're not asking for funding, you don't necessarily need to include it. However, I think it's helpful for new businesses to layout their financial projections anyway, just to see.

Essentially, what you're looking at is your prospective financial outlook for the next 5 years. If you're already established and selling goods, include your income statements, cash flow statements, and your balance sheets. If you have collateral you're going to be putting up against a loan, this is also where you include it.

Write out forecasted income statements – if you sell x

amount of product, you will make y after all expenses, for example – as well as your budgets and any prospective expenses.

Prospective expenses could be startup costs, which include initial ingredients to start, any equipment you need, packaging to sell your goods, and a marketing budget. Don't forget to include things like insurance (which you'll learn about in the next chapter), as well as any registration or permits you need to get your business off the ground.

YOUR ADDITIONAL SUPPORT DOCUMENTS

If you're using this business plan to obtain funding, a bank or individual investor might request additional information, like resumes, credit histories, or even licensing. This is where you put any of that. You also can add product pictures, contracts you've entered into within the business, and even letters of reference.

Once you have all of that worked out, you're going to put it all together, and you have a traditional business plan! I understand at this point in the book you are not ready to fully complete and flesh out your business plan.

After all, we haven't talked about licensing your business, marketing plans, or even nailing down your target market in detail.

Maybe you took my advice, and while you were reading this you jotted down potential goals or ideas. Come back to this chapter with those notes after you've finished the book and have a clearer picture of how you're going to run your business, and what those words even mean. Be sure to use the SMART system on all goals for yourself and your business, and be patient. Writing a business plan, well, it's not going to happen overnight!

REGISTERING YOUR BUSINESS AND LEGALITIES INVOLVED

I have said this before, but this is the biggest piece of advice I have for new and prospective business owners: always do things above board. Register your business, don't just take money and sell products. Have tax numbers, keep detailed records, and don't mess with the government. No one wants to get between the IRS and the taxes they are owed, after all.

I get it. This isn't a fun topic. It is much more fun to

talk about the recipes you're going to develop or the packaging you're going to use or even the social media strategies you'll implement to drive customers. But this is so important, so keep sticking with me for a while. Without all these legalities and regulations, you don't really have a business... you've got a hobby.

Keep in mind that just like with cottage food laws, where you live is going to change how you go about this. Some states have very cheap registration fees and almost no regulations, while others have a more complicated system that will have you visiting the local courthouse to get everything straight. I can't go into the rules for each and every state, that would be incredibly long. I can, however, tell you where to find the information and give you a good foundational understanding of how it all works.

The best advice I can give to you right now is to be patient. I know you're hyped about wanting to start your business, and I absolutely understand. However, this isn't going to happen overnight.

Much of this process is talking, sending details, and waiting. I get that the time you're spending on this could be used baking more, or developing recipes, or doing anything that will feel more like you're 'contributing' to the business, but this is just as important.

This takes time, but it's not complicated. And it's very, very important. So again, let's be patient when setting up your real, legitimate business.

THE FIRST STEP: REGISTERING YOUR BUSINESS

In order to become a legitimate business, you need to register your business. Make sense?

The first thing to do is to look at your state, city, and county. Just like I told you to look into your cottage food laws early into our book, you need to check out what special regulations your area has on businesses that sell food. If you can work out of your own kitchen, that's great, and it's going to save you some hassle – but if you need a commercial space, you may need to find that space before you register.

Contact your area health department, and talk about what regulations and standards they have. Some of it will be obvious, and just following basic food safety, while others may be more specific to that area. Take lots of notes, because a bad health department inspection can easily tank your business. Showing your willingness to learn, adapt, and abide by rules is just a huge plus in their book.

Okay, so you've got that out of the way – now, take a look at your state's official website. You're looking for what permits a bakery just like yours needs to get off the ground. State websites are surprisingly user-friendly, especially in the last few years when all of this was forced online, so you shouldn't have an issue. If you can't find anything on the state's website, Googling "Your State + Business Permits" is a good starting point. When I Google Ohio Business Permits, for example, I get the Ohio.gov page immediately that shows what licensing and permits I need, and how to register for them.

YOUR BUSINESS NAME

To register your business, you're going to need a name. If you're anything like me, you've probably already got the perfect name picked out, and it was what led the charge in the business. However, you need to make sure that your name is unique.

Do a Google search on your ideal business name. Are there any bakeries with that same name? Try variations, like a minor spelling change, to see what else shows up. Check social media, too, and search for your ideal name. If someone has already claimed that name, I would suggest you go back to the drawing board to protect yourself from future issues.

Once you've found a name that isn't obviously taken, go through your state's business records and search for your ideal name. Has anyone already beaten you to the punch, and registered your ideal name? What about a name that is super similar, with a similar business?

If you're in the clear, we can proceed to the next step. This may take a few tries. I personally had to go through a few different name ideas, each time falling in love with a funny or punny name just to realize I'm not as clever as I think I am, and someone else has thought of that name before. It was the first of many humbling experiences creating and building my business. Don't get discouraged!

REGISTER WITH THE STATE

For Ohio, like the majority of states, your first step is to register your information with the Secretary of State. These forms are available online, and are very easy to fill out. Fees range from $25 to over $100, depending on the type of business you're registering.

You also have to often register your name in Ohio, which is an additional $39. You can register your business under your actual business name, or under a trade name or fictitious name. This really doesn't apply to your type of business, because... why would you register under anything but your own name? It's really for businesses with multiple 'branches' wanting to present a different 'face', like how Nestle sort of owns the world but operates under many different 'names'. Make sense?

Note: Some states refer to this as a DBA, or *Doing Business As* registration!

REGISTERING FOR A BUSINESS TYPE

Alright, so there are a few different types of ownerships we're going to talk about. The type of ownership is important. The two main ones are an LLC, or a sole-proprietorship.

The easiest way to register is a sole-proprietorship.

And for many new business owners who don't understand what it really means, it has a lot of appeal. After all, you're the one and only owner. Why shouldn't your business reflect that? It's usually generally cheaper and easier to register as a sole-proprietorship, with fewer steps. The biggest benefit of this type of ownership is that you don't have to do separate business taxes or expenses, and it all gets rolled into your own personal taxes. In that way, it saves a lot of time.

However, I would discourage literally anyone, anywhere, from working under a sole proprietorship. The second business type is an LLC, and it's a much better option. While you do have to file more paperwork to set it up, and at the end of each tax season you do have to separate your business taxes from your personal taxes, it actually protects you as a person.

Basically, a Limited Liability Company, or LLC, says that this business is completely separate from you, the owner. If something awful happens and it goes under, you personally are not held responsible financially, just the business itself. If someone gets sick and dies due to your products, they cannot sue you as a person, just the company itself. If your business goes under and you have to liquidate, the bank can only come after the business for money, they cannot go after your own personal home (except in situations where it was placed as collateral for a loan, obviously) or vehicle. They can only go after the business's assets.

This layer of protection is absolutely essential for new businesses. The extra upfront work is more than worth that protection.

The only time I would ever even consider recommending a sole-proprietorship is when you are launching a very small business with no dream of expanding. If you just want to a side hustle to become above-board, and you never want to extend beyond that, perhaps a sole-proprietorship is worth it. Otherwise, take the extra steps and set up an LLC.

REGISTERING FOR AN LLC

Alright, now that we're in agreement, let's talk about how to go about setting up your very own LLC.

You're going to head to that place I sent you before, the website for your Secretary of State. You're specifically looking for something called The LLC Articles of Organization. Sometimes certain states will word it a little differently, but this is the gist of what you need.

Essentially, this form is your intent to form an LLC and proceed with your business. The vast majority of states now have these forms available online to download, fill out, and electronically return, but a few will still need you to pick it up or drop it off in person.

Download or otherwise acquire the form, and fill out all necessary details. It's all fairly basic – who you are, what your business is, that sort of thing. Rarely, you will also need to publish something called a 'notice of intention' in the local newspaper. This is crazy outdated, and most states are doing away with it, but if you are required to, be sure to do it as well so you don't miss an important step.

Finally, submit your fully completed form to the Secretary of State, along with the required fee. Again, this fee depends on the state – it can range from just $20 to over $100. This isn't a fee you can skip!

Some states will ask you to pay a corporate tax upfront, sort of like a promise. Others will let you wait until the normal tax time. If you're unclear on what you need to pay, contact your local Secretary of State's office and inquire. These folks handle this type of question every single day, and are usually more than willing to help out.

Finally, double-check that your state doesn't require you to pay or deal with an LLC Annual Report Fee. If this is something you'll have to deal with every year, well, that's annoying but it's just part of doing business in your state. It's better to be aware upfront than being surprised after.

Submit your forms to the local Secretary of State's office, submit any fee through their approved payment (mostly bank checks or money orders, but some now take credit cards or even cash in-person), and you're done.

Seriously, that's it! As long as your forms are approved, you have officially started your business journey as an established LLC, and you're ready for the next steps. Congratulations!

THE NITTY GRITTY OF STARTING YOUR BUSINESS, PART TWO

Now that you've established your business as an LLC, chosen a name, and registered properly, it's time to... well, do more registering. Specifically, let's talk about taxes.

Registering with the state isn't enough. You also have to register with the IRS so they know to expect money from you come tax time. You also need something called an EIN, or Employer Identification Number. Even if you're not planning on employing anyone but yourself, you still need to register for it.

In this chapter, we're also going to talk about how important business insurance is (spoiler alert: very!), as well as closing the chapter out with securing funding for your business, and the best ways to go about it. So many businesses are intimidated with funding, but none of this has to be scary or overwhelming!

Let's jump in and get you started!

TAXES: AN INEVITABLE

Once you've established your LLC, it's time to register with the IRS. You're going to need to obtain an EIN. As mentioned, even if you're not employing anyone else you need an EIN. However, all of this can easily and quickly be done online. You can get your own EIN without ever leaving your couch.

Open up the IRS website in a tab, and find your state's website from that. Fill out all of the information they require of you on the state application, but do not close that page. You're going to be redirected back to the IRS website after you fill out the state information. Open this in a new tab, and fill out the information there.

Once filled out on the IRS site, you can submit it and you'll immediately receive your EIN. Take that number and write it down. Keep that number safe! I recommend screenshotting it as well, just so you really can't lose it.

Go back to your tab from the state, and enter your EIN. Now you can submit and close those pages, because you're officially registered!

You need to also register with the state additionally as well. This will be either with the state's taxing authority or the revenue department, depending on your state. Your goods may also be subjected to sales tax, and you'll need to apply for a tax seller's permit with your state. Your state's Department of Revenue site should also be able to get you that form!

I've said this before, but I really just want to take a moment to nail this home. You not only need to do everything above – register with your state, register with the IRS, etc., but you need to follow all local laws, too. Your city or county may have specific laws.

For example, you need to check with your community before starting your business out of your home. If you're not using a commercial kitchen and instead of working from your home kitchen, there may be rules or regulations in your county or even within your HOA (Home Owners Association) about starting a business in the home. You need to check with all local regulations as well – a quick call or email to your local government offices should be enough.

Skirting around local laws is never recommended. You may incur fines and disruptions to your business that will cost you a lot more in the long run.

As a business owner, you're going to have to deal with taxes related to the business. You can't ignore it, or hope to 'figure it out' in April when tax time comes. It's absolutely imperative that you follow through with business taxes.

Depending on the size of your business, you may only have a pay a portion of the taxes you owe. If you're a small business, you also may qualify for something called the Qualified Business Income Deduction. This essentially takes 20% off of the qualified income you make that year, and you don't pay taxes on this. For a small business, this really makes a difference, so be sure to investigate if your business does fall under this umbrella.

WHAT ARE SELF-EMPLOYMENT TAXES, AND DO I HAVE TO PAY THEM?

Here's the deal – you may not be employing anyone else but yourself. However, even if you're the only one slaving away to make your business a success, you still need to pay something called a self-employment tax. Even if you're the owner, you're also an employee of the company.

This money essentially just pays into both Medicare and Social Security, and is based on the income of the business. You can't get around paying this.

PAYING QUARTERLY

Running a business is different from just doing your home taxes. When you do your own personal taxes, you probably pay (or get back) each year, once a year. However, businesses are held to different standards, and must pay towards their estimated taxes each quarter.

If you do not pay your estimated taxes each quarter, the IRS can and will fine you for a lack of payment. If you are in a state that will require your customers to pay sales tax on your goods as well, you will have to set up a system to report the tax to the state and pay that each quarter as well. Each state is going to have a different system to record your sales and pay into it.

There are also two different types of taxes you're going to need to keep in mind. One is a state income tax, and the other is something called a gross receipt tax. The vast majority of states will only ever have to deal with a state income tax, but there are a few state exceptions.

If you went against my strong suggestion and chose a sole-proprietorship instead of an LLC, you may not have to pay this.

BE SURE TO WRITE IT ALL OFF

If you've never run a business before, you may not realize how great it is to write off certain items. However, there are many things you're already paying for that you can consider a business expense.

Your phone bill, for example, if you're using your

phone, can be considered a business expense for tax deductions. So can your internet bill, any travel expenses you're incurring for the business, and any home office expenses if you're doing work for the business out of the office. If you have to buy a new computer for your business, a new monitor, a new desk... all of this is tax-deductible.

Business meals are also considered tax-deductible, as well as business insurance, which we'll talk about soon. The key thing to know is that you need to keep all of the receipts for any expenses that are directly related to the business.

MAINTAINING GOOD MANUFACTURING STANDARDS: OR, USE COMMON SENSE

I don't know your personal background. I don't know if you have ever even worked in a professional kitchen or bakery before. If you have, most of this stuff is going to be common sense to you – but in my experience, it's different for folks who are running their own business, too.

Maintaining good manufacturing standards is so important when you're running any business and making products, but exceptionally important when we're talking about food safety. Food safety and health is so, so vital, and one mistake really can cost you your business.

I don't want to scare you, but it's that important.

There are some basic things you need to abide by not just for health code, but for your customers safety. I go into all of this later in the book, but I want you to keep it in mind. If you're not sure about good operating procedures, and you can't tour a professional bakery or kitchen, consider watching one of those cheesy shows. Kitchen Nightmares with Gordon Ramsey is a lot, but his investigations into kitchens and how they run really can show you what not to do. The same with Bar Rescue, with episodes that include a kitchen.

Some things to remember:

Everything opened should have a label with a date of when it was opened. Use half a butter container? Label and date it. Used a portion of sugar, or flour? Label, date, and store in an airtight container. Saving half a container of buttercream for tomorrow? You guessed it – label and date it.

These little things may seem silly, because you're the one using them, and you know when you opened something up. But at a certain point, your production may get to the place where you are so busy you can't remember when you opened or used something. The labeling and dating of the product is going to save you a lot of headache in that regard.

In addition, it's simply required by law! Proper labels, with the proper dates, are required, because you cannot sell something once it's past date.

Storage is also important. You can't simply toss a half-used, unsealed container in the fridge overnight and think it's fine. Check out restaurant supply websites or stores to get an idea of how a professional bakery or restaurant stores their goods – these exist for a reason, not just to get you to spend money!

Proper sanitation between batch production is also vital, and something the health department looks for. After making a batch of vanilla icing, for example, you can't simply put that dirty bowl back on the mixer and start making chocolate. You need to sanitize the area and the equipment.

Properly sterilizing your area is also something the health department regularly looks for. When I worked in a restaurant as a kid, we called them 'Sani Buckets,' but they are really just designated sanitizer buckets filled with a food-safe sanitizer, and anytime you are done with an area or workspace, the entire workspace gets cleaned with that sanitizer solution. Countertops, equipment, etc. Not only does it keep it sterile, the area also simply looks better and cleaner.

The FDA also requires proper labeling and identification of utensils, scoops, and containers. This may be less of a 'big deal' in a bakery because you don't have to worry about cross-contamination of raw foods like chicken or beef, but it's still important. All containers and utensils should be color-coded so you immediately know what to use when. For example, only green-lidded containers and green-handled scoops should be used when working with an allergen. All recycling goes into yellow containers. Use what colors you have and feel comfortable with, but always stick with colored labels.

In general, cleanliness is king within a kitchen. Not just your countertops and tools, but floors, walls, and more. Your kitchen, at all times, should be clean. It can be cluttered or messy (though I do not recommend it, we've all had those weeks), but it must always be clean. If you're not clear as to why, be sure to watch a few episodes of Kitchen Nightmares with Gordon Ramsey. Seriously, this is a real suggestion – while a lot of the show is set for shock value, it can teach you about food safety and proper kitchen technique.

A big part of proper manufacturing practices is documentation. As you start building your business and creating recipes, you should have written steps not only for each recipe, but for cleaning, opening the kitchen, closing the kitchen, etc. Everything you do should be documented, with clear steps. If you had to step away from your kitchen for whatever reason, someone else should be able to look at all of your documentation and know exactly how to run and maintain your kitchen.

I'm going to go into this in a lot more detail later, so hang tight. I can't stress enough how important it is for you to keep good safety procedures when handling food. At best, not following proper food safety will get you fined. At worst? You could literally kill someone. I'm not exaggerating, and you'll see why soon.

BUSINESS INSURANCE

For your safety, the safety of your business, and your own personal peace of mind, you need business insurance. I have met folks who say that they skimped or skipped business insurance entirely because they couldn't afford it or couldn't justify it, and it blows my mind every time.

I understand insurance is expensive, and might seem like something "nice to have, but not needed." However, many states require a certain level of insurance for any business. In addition, you will never regret paying for insurance once you actually have to use it.

There are a few types of insurance you're going to run into in the business world, so we'll talk about those.

Commercial Property Insurance is the insurance that covers the loss or damage of the business's property. This could include equipment, goods, and sometimes carries a small amount of liability in case someone else gets hurt. If you're working out of a commercial space, check with your landlord to find out what their own insurance covers, because you may fall under that umbrella.

Product Liability Insurance is insurance that covers you in the event of financial loss due to an issue with a product. If you purchase a bad batch of something, or something happens and you need to get rid of your product, product liability insurance may cover that. You need to have a detailed, engaged conversation with your insurance agent, however, because most policies require you to have your good manufacturing processes on file with them, and you need to prove you know and follow them in case of something happening. Knowing and following your insurance regulations will make sure if you do need to make a claim, they will cover you properly.

If you're working out of your home, there may be limited coverage from your homeowner's insurance or rental insurance, but you must consult your insurance company even if there isn't. In some situations, your homeowner's insurance may be void if you did not inform them you are running a business from your home. Seriously, don't mess with it, and be sure to do your research.

I get that for many people, insurance may be just as overwhelming as taxes or registering your business. The best advice I can impart if you feel like that is to take it slow and talk to several different insurance companies that offer business insurance. Ask lots of questions, and understand the coverage entirely before you sign anything.

MO' MONEY, MO' PROBLEMS: FUNDING, LOANS, AND MORE

Here's some real nitty-gritty talk: money is going to be the biggest thing in your business, by far. You may already know that, but your mind perhaps doesn't quite understand what I mean. Money is going to drive every single aspect of your business. Not baking, not customers, not growing, but money.

Opening a bank account, securing funding, and generating revenue are all overwhelming to someone who hasn't opened a business before. While I do not know the exact specifications of your business, I can offer you lots of guidance in how I did it, how I recommend new businesses do it, and what to look for.

It doesn't have to be complicated, but you should feel confident with your decisions.

OPENING A BANK ACCOUNT

The first step is to open a business bank account. This is different from a personal bank account, and you should not attach your business account to your personal account in any way. You can use the same bank you do your personal banking, but you shouldn't default to them. Consult with local banks in the area to determine who has the best small business programs.

Many times, this will be a local credit union, believe it or not. Don't discount the smaller banks, especially if there is one that is close to your home or business location. Other than good interest rates, bank deals, and customer service, you should keep in mind hours. If you are going to be going TO the bank to deposit money, you're going to need a bank with hours that work with you. Some smaller local banks may only be open a few hours a day, which is not ideal.

Finally, be sure to consider ease of use. Not just visiting, but using the website. Do they have an app? Does it work, or does it just sort of exist? How detailed of records can they produce for you, including income, spending, and more? You should be keeping your own records outside of the bank account, but accessing this information quickly and easily is fantastic. Having an easy-to-use bank app and website will make banking overall a much easier experience.

BANKING LINE OF CREDIT

Most banks that handle business accounts offer a business line of credit to qualifying accounts and businesses. This is not a loan, but more like a credit card. You may get certain perks for using it, and an interest rate. If you don't pay off your bills each month, you will obviously incur interest and fees.

I highly recommend having a line of credit for your business. However, you need to use it responsibly. It's there as a safety net, and perhaps to gain bonuses from use. It's not "free money," and you need to keep track of all your business expenses closely and be smart with your spending.

A business line of credit is a really, really great way to help prevent being overwhelmed by unexpected costs. If you end up having to repair a piece of equipment, replace that equipment, or otherwise need money upfront, a business line of credit can help prevent disaster.

If you don't need a ton of capital to get your business up and running, and you want a small safety net, a line of credit may be the best and easiest option for you.

BANKING LOANS

Different from a line of credit is a banking loan, which is... well, a loan. You agree to borrow a set amount of money for a set amount of time, and you need to pay a portion of it back each month until you have paid the loan in full, plus whatever interest you also agree to.

If you need a more considerable amount of capital to get your business running – perhaps you need money for equipment, startup costs, or to float yourself in a standing location until you make revenue.

Your credit, and your business's credit, will obviously factor into your interest rate. Most traditional business loans offer an interest of 5-8%, with repayment anywhere from 3 to 10 years, depending on the loan, the bank, and the business. A traditional loan, though, isn't fast – it can take six months or more from the time you apply for the loan to the time you get the money.

IS AN SBA LOAN FOR ME?

The SBA, or the US Small Business Administration, is a piece of the government set aside to help small businesses like you grow and expand. The SBA works essentially like a middle man, not like a bank. When you receive an SBA loan, you're not getting government money. Instead, you're working with a partner approved and vetted by the government to help businesses with borderline credit who wouldn't otherwise be able to access bank loans.

Interest rates vary, but are usually 6-8%, a little higher than a traditional bank loan. However, as I mentioned, if you have questionable or minimal credit, an SBA loan might still offer a better interest rate.

SBA also boasts unique benefits you may not be able to find elsewhere, like lower down payments and minimal to no collateral. If you're struggling, the SBA also offers programs for small business owners to help grow and thrive in your new role as a business owner. There is even something called a "microloan" program, which promises to help provide small businesses $50,000 or less in loans to start their growth. For some bakeries, this might be all you need.

Some SBA loans can, again, take as long as 6 months – but some take as little as 36 hours after approval to get the funds. It can vary wildly depending on the type of loan you need and the amount of money you require.

BE WARY OF MID-PRIME ALTERNATIVE

I've seen numerous folks get bitten by the business bug, and make some bad decisions regarding funding. They almost always involve something called a mid-prime alternative business loan. Think about this type of loan like a paycheck advance place, but for businesses instead.

They almost exclusively target and cater to businesses and organizations with lower credit (sub-650), or businesses that don't have the documentation or experience needed to secure a traditional loan.

The benefit of these types of loans is that they're simple. I'm not going to say anyone can secure one, but it doesn't come with a lot of hoops to jump through like a more strict bank loan. You also get your cash within a week or two, so for those that are very impatient, that's a big plus.

The downside? Interest rates can be brutal, ranging anywhere from 8% all the way up to 20% or more. Repayment can be due in as little as 18 months, or run upwards of 5 years. 5 years sounds ideal... until you think about all that interest you're paying for that time frame.

If you need money quickly, this is an option. If you have zero credit and you're determined to succeed, I'm not going to tell you not to go into this type of loan. It's really not my place, honestly. But you need to be extremely careful, and ensure you can pay this loan back on time.

Sometimes, this is used as a bridge loan, or temporary capital to float your business until your full banking loan comes through.

MERCHANT CASH ADVANCE

To the tune of, be careful, we have our final loan option: something called a merchant cash advance. Sometimes also referred to as a business cash advance, this essentially lets small businesses receive an 'advance' on capital, allowing them to buy inventory or purchase equipment.

Bad credit is generally not a problem, but the rates are outrageous. I've seen an MCA with interest rates as high as 100%... seriously. You usually get your money within a week, and the payback term is very short, generally less than 18 months.

This is also sometimes used as a bridge loan, to fill a gap until more permanent financing is available. This is so dangerous in my opinion, as it can put you – and your business – in a very tight financial spot. However, it is an option, and as long as you have a payback plan in place, it could be reasonable for your business.

CROWDFUNDING

I have never, personally funding a bakery or enterprise

through crowdfunding. Of course, websites like Go Fund Me also weren't around when I first started out, so I'm sure that has something to do with it, too. The principle is the same as below, finding investors, but you are reaching a much wider audience.

Platforms like Kickstarter, IndieGoGo, and Go Fund Me are all places that let you set up what are essentially 'donations' to help fund your business. Sometimes there is a fee, and often you are asked to provide something in return. For example, you could offer that everyone who puts $100 towards your bakery venture gets free drip coffee once a day for six months.

Funding for something like this is often slow, and it relies heavily on you knowing people who want to contribute, or being able to spread the word to people who may. However, you also potentially get great exposure and can share more about your love of baking and passion, potentially driving customers to you when you do open.

INVESTORS

Thinking about bringing investors on? It's a little

different from crowdfunding, above, but the core principle is the same – you are exchanging something for something else. If you're interested in exchanging equity (or, ownership in your bakery business) for investments, there are websites like AngelList, Seedinvest, WeFunder, CircleUp, and StartEngine that may be able to help. Don't just spam your bakery on all of these – read the fine print, and really consider how much you're willing to give up, and for what.

You should consider, however, looking for investors locally. If your focus is a specific area, it tracks that your investor would also be in that area, looking to help grow the community.

Attending community events, especially if you can get your goods into the hands of potential investors, is big. Ask friends and family, think about the powerful or wealthy folks you know that may be interested, or consider where you can go to meet these people, even if that place is online, on LinkedIn or Facebook.

Finding an investor locally is a game of who you know, which is frustrating for the less than connected folks reading this, but it's just the way it is. Outside investors, with less connection to your town or business, might be easier to find.

THINK ABOUT RENTING

Not related to bank loans at all is renting equipment. So many bakers want to dive into their business with brand new (or gently used, as I did) equipment, but leasing or renting your equipment might save you a ton of overhead at first.

While you do pay more in the long run, it gives you a chance to try out equipment that might not be available to you otherwise. And you could figure out that in six months, this piece of equipment isn't needed at all, saving you money.

I recommend renting or leasing equipment if you have no other choice, without a doubt. The upfront cost is a lot smaller, and as you grow you can put aside the lease and purchase the piece of equipment when you know you need it. This is a reasonable way to handle 'big' purchases that you can't afford otherwise, without being hit with a crazy high-interest rate.

WHAT YOU'LL NEED, FOR SURE

The most important thing you're going to need is a business plan, which you should have started crafting at the beginning of the last chapter... did you? It's okay, you can come back to that chapter.

Your business plan really is the key to unlocking investments, even loans. Showing the bank, potential investors, or even family who want to help see your dream succeed how serious you are starts with a well-crafted business plan. Take your time, compile as much data as you can, and don't be afraid to go back and add onto it.

Your personal credit score, as well as your business's credit score, also matter. The lower your score, the less likely someone is going to volunteer to give you lots of money. "Why does my personal credit score matter?" You might be wondering.

Lenders aren't just looking at how you're going to manage your business, they're also looking at how you – the personnel at the helm of the ship, so to speak – will manage debt. If you have a poor credit score, I'm not here to judge, but you should know it may show banks you struggle to juggle payments and debt situations.

You can obtain a free copy of your credit report from Annual Credit Report, and NerdWallet will offer you a free credit score, if you're unsure of where you stand personally. There are tons of resources out there for improving your personal credit, disputing incorrect charges, and getting your score where you need it to be. I could write a whole book on this, but let's be honest – I'm not a financial or credit score expert, just someone that has run a successful business and has been there before.

You're going to need lots of documents, both legal and financial. It might feel overwhelming gathering these, so give yourself plenty of time. Some basic requirements for most loans or lines of credit include:

Balance sheet and income statements from the business, if applicable

Personal and business tax returns, often from several years prior

Personal and business bank statements

Copies of any leases related to the business

Copies of any licenses the business holds

The articles of incorporation, and any other legal registration you have done for your business

A photo of your license or passport, to prove you're you

A resume that shows why you're qualified to run your business, and what you bring to the table. You may also want or need to include the resumes of any additional staff, especially if they bring something special to the table.

Financial projections, especially if you have a limited operating history.

Always know the minimum qualifications or requirements for a loan before you apply for a loan. There's nothing worse than gathering a ton of information, talking to a banker for weeks, and filling out numerous forms before realizing that you don't qualify for one reason or the other. Sometimes it's that you haven't been in business long enough – sometimes, too long. Sometimes it's that your credit score isn't good enough, or sometimes that you have a lingering loan from the bank or another organization.

Do I Need Collateral?

Great question! I've skirted around this issue, but in most cases for a larger loan, you're going to need some type of collateral against the loan. For an SBA loan above $25,000, you are required to put down both collateral and a personal guarantee from every single owner of the business that holds 20% or more. This personal guarantee places your personal credit score and your personal assets against that loan.

Sometimes lenders only want one or the other – you may not have to put collateral if you're willing to put a personal guarantee down, for example. Others may take a lien on all your business assets until your loan is paid off, which you could argue is just another form of collateral. This would give the lender the right to seize your business assets, like inventory and equipment, in the event you default.

It's up to you as to what is most 'worth it.' It's going to depend a lot on what you have to offer as collateral, how much you're asking for, and what lender you are going through.

EQUIPMENT YOU'LL NEED

While we're thinking about money, let's discuss what equipment you're going to probably need. Behind something like rent, the equipment you're going to be using is the biggest expense a traditional bakery needs. I read an article a few years ago from an experienced baker who was opening her third location, and the equipment for that location ran about $150,000. Depending on what you're buying, and how large your bakery operation will be, you could spend a lot less... or a lot more.

I've mentioned before that buying used saved me a ton of money in the long run, and I think you should consider looking at used equipment for at least some of your products. A bakery case, for example, should probably be purchased new because you don't know what was stored previously, or how it was cleaned. Lingering stains or smells are not what you're looking for, after all.

Inspect all of your equipment thoroughly, and test it if at all possible. Inquire on what it was used for, if they have serving history for the equipment, and how old it was. A smaller diner-style restaurant might have an oven that was used a lot less than a previous bakery selling off used equipment.

This isn't a comprehensive list, but here are some things you need to be considering.

Professional grade mixer: There are a few options for you. If you'll be doing cookies or cakes, a cake mixer may be all you need. They range in size from just 5 quarts (the size in my personal kitchen!) all the way up to 140 quarts. Often for smaller bakeries, a countertop model is ideal. If you'll be making huge batches of the same thing, a floor mixer might be better for you. If you're mostly making sturdy, hardy doughs, like bread doughs or even bagels, a dough mixer is probably best. These have an intense workhorse motor that can handle the repeated abuse of a tough dough.

Dishwasher (trust me, washing that many dishes by hand is not fun. It's possible with a 3 station sink, but it's not an enjoyable experience)

Large work benches, for lots of space to spread out and work: You have a variety of options here depending on the size of your space. Bakers tables are great, especially mobile ones that can lock in place, but not all kitchens have space for them. You're looking for enough countertop real estate to handle all of your baking, ideally with storage underneath. Wooden tops or stainless steel are both good options.

Bakery case: There are both bakery cases that offer refrigeration, and ones that simply hold the goods. You can find ones that only staff can access, or ones with front access. Find a bakery case that fits in your space, but doesn't overwhelm it.

Traditional ovens: Consider how you're going to use your oven, and what you'll be making. A convection oven with rotating racks is awesome for cookies, but not at all ideal for delicate items like souffles. A deck oven is great if you'll be making a lot of breads or cakes.

Proofing oven, for proofing yeasted doughs.

Racks: Sometimes called speed racks or proofing racks, you need enough racks – with trays that fit – to hold products while they cool, or while they are in their final rise before baking. Some racks are stationary, while others have wheels that can be moved. Some are smaller, holding only half-sized baking sheets, while others hold full-sized. I also recommend a rack cover to help keep dust and debris out of the goods. Pick up an insulated one or two for extra help rising, especially if you're not using a proofing oven.

"Smallwares": These are basically all the "little" things you need to make your bakery function. Sifters, baking sheet liners, spoons, spatulas, rolling pins, piping bags, measuring cups and spoons (so many measuring cups!), cake pans, bread pans, muffins pans, pie pans, bench scrapers... you get the drift. Make a list of everything you think you're going to need in order to bake all of the things you want.

Storage: Storage is important, and you can rarely have enough! Food boxes with airtight lids and ingredient bins are going to become your best friend. Use something like a dunnage rack to hold everything off the ground, staying in compliance with the health code.

Furnishings: If you're going to have a traditional bakery, you're going to need some traditional furnishing. Many folks don't take into consideration how expensive quality seating or even something like light fixtures are, so be sure to calculate that properly.

Remodeling: If you're setting up an in-person location, either a traditional café or a takeaway location, there's a good chance you're going to have to put some money back into your business. I'm not talking about small things, like a chair or a lamp, but big things. Paint, electrical, even moving walls. Calculating how much work your space is going to need and how much that will cost is vital to your success, short term.

Extras: Are you serving coffee? You're going to need, at minimum, a basic drip coffee machine. However, depending on your target market, you may need to expand into the coffee shop side of things, with espresso and freshly ground beans. This can add up quickly, as quality espresso machines are not cheap. Most customers, however, expect this from a hip and new bakery.

Once again, I'm going to recommend a list. I know, I know, I make a lot of lists – but being organized and having everything together when you're starting a business is a huge deal, and will save you time, money, and a lot of stress down the line

You should have a want and a need column in your list, and organize what you're going to need to get your bakery off the ground. If you're doing an in-person bakery, you're probably going to have a lot more on your need list, like furnishings or coffee equipment.

Once you have your list, it's time to start doing research. What size mixer are you going to need, based on the items you want to sell? What smallwares will you need for your business? If you're just crafting specialty wedding cakes, you won't need as many as a café style bakery with cupcakes, muffins, and cookies.

Put a price next to each item, or at least a ballpark price. You can even have two, if you'd like – one for a new item, and one for a used professional-grade item.

This is a lot of work, but you can do it bit by bit, when you have time to step away from other things in your life. This list, and even rough pricing for each item, is going to make it a lot easier to estimate how much funding you need, how much money you need saved, and what upfront expenses you can expect to face. Going into this business blind is not something I recommend.

TARGET MARKET, BRANDING, AND NAMING: THE FUN PART

Your name, and your branding, is so very important. You know when you get a Starbucks cup, for example, exactly what you're getting by the logo. Their packaging is identifiable immediately to what they're selling, and their brand.

The same goes for so many different brands. Apple, for example, has built its brand upon minimalistic designs, clean lines, and its signature logo. Coca-Cola also has a huge global branding plan, so that even if you are overseas, you know immediately you're holding a bottle of Coke. You know what to expect.

So how do you pick a good name? How do you brand yourself properly? And, let's dig further – how do you target your branding to your target market? How do you identify a target market at all?!

We've had a few chapters of 'boring' stuff, like taxes and legal stuff. Let's dive into some of the more enjoyable and motivating aspects of creating your business.

NAIL DOWN YOUR TARGET MARKET

On one hand, you really want your bakery to appeal to a lot of people, especially if you're a more traditional bakery with a storefront, either a café style or a takeout-only business. However, you should also have a target market.

A target market is essentially your ideal customer. Who you're marketing and selling to the most. Who is going to be buying your goods?

If you're an online-only business, this is probably even

more important to nail down, but you really should have an idea of who you're selling to before you get any further.

Grab a piece of paper and a pen, or pull up a document on your computer or phone. Ask yourself a series of questions when you're thinking about your target market, and write down the answers to help nail down specifics.

Who is your ideal customer?

What is their age, or age range?

What is their occupation? What does that make their annual salary? How much disposable income do they have?

What does your ideal customer do during their time off work?

What education does your ideal customer have?

Where do they live, and how are they going to access your products?

Is your ideal customer single? Married? In a relationship?

Sounds silly when we're talking about baked goods, but stick with me. If your bakery is selling to the local college crowd, they probably have a part-time job at most, and a limited budget. They can't afford the premium price that over-the-top packaging will entail, and may appreciate a more toned-down experience.

On the flip side, if you're putting your bakery in a posh downtown location, or you're selling to high-end business folks in an office park, you're going to be able to charge a premium for a premium product. These are the people that will expect a higher quality product, including packaging and branding, and they are often willing and able to pay for that product.

Knowing the answers to at least some of these questions will make your final product that much easier to sell, honestly.

Spend some time really thinking about this, because it's important. You're going to have to keep the area you want your bakery in mind when figuring out a target market if you're planning on a traditional bakery – you're not going to attract a high-end crowd if you're smack dab in the middle of a questionable neighborhood, and college kids aren't going to flock to a bakery in the suburbs if there are options closer to campus and nightlife.

Once you've got some answers to these questions, ask yourself a few more questions.

Does my target market make sense for my products?

Are there enough people in my target market or my ideal area to support my business?

Do these people have a need for my product? Can they afford my product?

Are there markets similar to mine that are overlooked that I can target?

How easily can I reach my target market?

You should know all the answers to this question. These may not come immediately – in fact, you should let it really marinade and take your time, do some research. What baked goods are popular in your area? What do local bakeries sell, and what did you struggle to find? As you figure out your niche and what you're going to be selling, your target market will follow.

DON'T FEEL BAD IF YOU HAVE TO SHIFT FOCUS

Did you have a target market in mind before realizing that they're actually not perfect for your business? Did you have your heart set on a location or demographic, just to realize that the market is oversaturated, or they don't have the interest, money, or time for your product?

That's okay. In the business world, you're going to run into a ton of trial and error. There will be many times that you are going to struggle to find the right path, and it's completely possible that you're not going to knock it out of the park the first time.

Don't beat yourself up! Sit down, be bummed for a minute, then shake it off and try again. You're going to be doing this a lot in your journey as a business owner, so the sooner you can pivot and try again, the better off you're going to be.

FIND WHAT'S MISSING

I've alluded to this previously, but when you're creating your bakery I really want you to think about not just what you can do, and do well, but what is missing from your market.

Is there nowhere in town to get really excellent, fresh bagels? Maybe the choices for fresh bread are aggressively lacking? Is there no small café to get a fresh muffin and a cup of coffee while you study, work, or just relax?

This is called positioning, and it's basically finding a hole and then filling it. Even if bagels, or fresh bread, isn't the core of your business, if you can find a hole in the market and fill it people will still be drawn to your business.

Does that make sense?

Note: For many of us, starting a business like a bakery is because you do something really well, and you have a passion and desire to share that specific thing. With positioning, it almost seems impersonal, like you're just filling a hole and not really creating from love.

It's important to remember that by positioning yourself properly in the market, you can do that thing you're passionate about, while also paying the bills and being successful.

BRANDING: WHAT IT IS, WHY IT MATTERS

A lot of newer business owners struggle with branding, with many of them not really taking it seriously. But real, serious businesses have good branding, and it's important for your business to be taken seriously. I've mentioned it before, but this is the type of thing that separates a home hobby baker from a real, serious business.

Branding is a huge part of your business. It's more than just packaging, or signs, but it's also marketing, and persona. Think about your brand as your identity as a company, the core and central part of your business. From that core everything happens – marketing, packaging, website design, even your design aesthetic within your kitchen or bakery.

Branding is everything.

When you're coming up with your branding concepts and working on them, I want you to keep in mind your target market. Is this something that your target market will appreciate? Is this something they want or need?

Also keep in mind your story and your brand's identity. Is this branding in line with your story? Are you making a connection? Does it all fit together? If you're making a branding decision that doesn't align with your story of why you started your bakery, or won't appeal to your target market, you're making the wrong choice.

Let's figure out your story, and the persona you put in front of your customers.

AVOID NEGATIVITY

This is yet again one of those sections that I shouldn't have to write, but I'm writing it out of experience. There are a surprising number of small businesses that make this mistake, but you never want to base your business on negativity of any kind.

No one wants to support a business that is based on negativity. You don't want that sort of energy or mood infecting your business, or your customers. When you're creating branding, or writing out your business story, or even sharing things about your business, you always want to focus on the positive.

In short: be positive, don't get caught up in internet

culture or "cancel culture", and don't try to push the envelope to be funny or edge-y. While I would never tell you to compromise your morals or beliefs, especially as a business, you need to find that line.

Okay, now that we have that done, let's take our first steps to nail down our branding.

OUR STORY

In your notebook, I'm going to ask you to write some things down. I'll ask a series of questions, and it's up to you to write down your answers. These questions are to help figure out your business's direction, your story as a business, and to start shaping your story. Yes, this matters for your branding – it's all connected!

I recommend putting your polished story on your website, for visitors to see and understand just who you are and what you're about. People like connecting with brands they're familiar with, and if they feel a connection with you, they're more likely to continue purchasing products from you. Brand loyalty is real.

Who are you? You, the business owner, the person behind the brand? There's a good chance if you're reading this, you're not starting a bakery business with a million dollars of financial banking and a huge team of investors and voices. You're you, doing this your way. People want to know about the person behind the small business.

What is it you do? You bake, obviously. But what products do you have to sell? What are you making? What lines of products, how do you plan to expand? What is the reason you got into baking in the first place? Has it always been a passion? Did you discover your talent and skill later in life? Talk about it!

Who do you bake for? This is sort of touching on your target market, here. Who do you want to bake for? Who do you want to buy your products? Who are you trying to help support, or reach?

Why do you do it? This is really where you want to talk about your motivations? Why do you care about baking, about the community, etc.? What drove you to your target market? To this business?

How do you do it? I'm not telling you to share trade secrets or anything, but talk a little bit about your process. How do you bake your goods? Where do you work from, and what health assurances do you make? How do you choose your recipes, your ingredients, your designs?

What's in your future? Where do you see your business in a year? Five years? Even longer? You can touch on your hopes, dreams, short and long-term goals for the business, and even talk about how you plan to achieve them.

You don't need to make your story long – a few paragraphs at most! – but a quick blurb about you, your story, and your passion will go a long way.

Your story should be personal, and your readers should feel a connection to it. This will help you stand out from the crowd, and build a connection. It should be authentic. It does not necessarily have to be 100% true, but you should never, ever just go to a competitor's site or store and pull their story.

It's important to remember that there is more competition than ever, and building those connections with your customers is really going to make a difference. There are so many big box stores or options for consumers to get their goods – make sure that you're their first choice.

Note: Don't be afraid to get emotional or personal!

Humans crave connections, and so many people like supporting small or local businesses because they are able to form those connections. I cannot stress this point enough!

BRANDING THE PRODUCTS

At this point you should at least have the outline of your personal business story, including what the business means to you, the owner, and why you are going to be successful. You also have established your target market, who they are, and what they are interested in. Now let's touch on the more obvious parts of branding.

Your company name is a big part of this. You probably have an idea for the name, or perhaps you maybe have already established your business in that name. Awesome! If you haven't hit that yet, though, let's talk about it anyway.

Does your name convey what it should? Does it fit into your target market? Do you identify with the name, or does someone within your target market identify with it? What does your name say about your story, your branding, your company as a whole? If you're concerned about any part of those questions, take a step back and reconsider.

Be sure to not try and get too clever with your name, or any part of your main marketing. If it's hard to spell, to remember, or annoys your market, you're going to be turning off your customers before they even place your first order and taste your goods.

Logos are another big, big part of your branding. Take a minute to think about all the famous brands that are so well known – I mentioned brands like Coke and Apple before, but Microsoft, Sony, even 'newer' companies like AirBnB, Casper, or Dropbox. Their logo is clear, easy to identify, and fits in very well with the rest of their branding.

If you're not a graphic artist or you don't have experience with designing logos, consider reaching out to a professional. If you have a concept or direction to give them, even better! Think about other, similar logos you love, and what you value in your logos and your design.

Something simple, clean, and easily identifiable as yours is important.

You can hire a graphic artist online for not as much as you may be expecting! Fivver, UpWorks, and Guru are all great choices for you. Go into the process with an open mind, but a list of examples options for them to work with. This is going to help you get the perfect final product.

YOUR PACKAGING MATTERS

The packaging that you put your products into matters, and should be on brand. However, it also needs to fit with your target market.

If you're catering to a higher-end customer that values the higher touches, a higher-end packaging isn't just a nice addition – it is really a must. These types of customers value those things, even if they cost a little bit more.

Consider what you're putting your baked goods in, Look into getting your logo on bags, boxes, and even tissue paper. Whatever you're giving your customers, if you can put your logo on it, do! It may be more expensive, but again, your clientele is looking for that higher touch.

If you're catering to a budget crowd, these extra touches matter a lot less. Focusing on keeping your prices down for your college-aged students, for example, might mean going with a more generic box or bag. That's okay! You need to know what your target market cares about in order to make these decisions, though. Just one of the many reasons knowing your target market and who is going to be buying your products matters.

Note: I wish I had thought of this sooner, when I was just starting out and stringing together a budget. If you really can't afford 'fancy' packaging, that's okay! Consider doing the next best thing: getting a stamp.

Have a custom stamp made for your business, with your logo, and a couple of containers of ink that matches your brandings color scheme. For each box you package, slap that stamp across the top.

It's a super cheap way to give your packaging a higher touch, without that big price tag.

MARKET RESEARCH: THE FAST TRACK

Learning all about market research is important, but

again – it's one of those things you could really write a whole book about. However, you don't really need to know everything about market research under the sun in order to properly do research for your own business.

In fact, we've already talked about it some – finding information about your own target market! That is the first step to doing market research for your brand new business.

Note: Market research can be tedious, boring, and even daunting to some folks. However, it's such an important part of building a business. You should never go into your business completely blind, not knowing who you're selling to, how they buy things, and more.

Sometimes business owners can luck out and simply stumble

THE DIFFERENCE BETWEEN PRIMARY AND SECONDARY MARKET RESEARCH

When you're learning about research in school, they teach you the difference between primary and secondary market research. This isn't super important, but you should organize any research you're doing for your business into these two main categories.

Primary research is from a primary source. It's all first-hand information about your market, your customers, and your area.

Secondary research is a little more removed. Instead of hearing something directly from the source, you're getting a second hand account. That can be trend reports, industry content from blogs or reports, sales data, that sort of thing.

Both are important, but for different reasons. Primary research is the best way to get real insight into your target market and what they say they want and need. "From the horse's mouth", so to speak. However, secondary research is also very important, but in a different way. No matter how many people say they want to switch to organic, or compost, if they're not doing it, it doesn't matter. Does that make sense?

Secondary research can tell the facts, straight up. You get more raw, hard numbers with secondary research. It's less idealization and wishful thinking.

The best starting place to find research on your area,

your local demographics, and your target market, in general, is the government! No surprise, the government keeps a pretty close eye on most folks – and they offer that information for us to use, too. I've mentioned it briefly before, but the US Census Bureau is the place to start when you're looking for information about your demographic. The Bureau of Labor and Statistics can also be incredibly helpful.

You really want to gather all the information you possibly can. This is exceptionally important if you have a physical location, because you really want to know all about the folks who live, work, and visit the area you're located at – but the information in general on your ideal target market is just as vital, even if you're selling online.

There are also commercial sources, which are usually a little harder to gather. Agencies like Pew or Gartner regularly conduct market research and publish their findings, but you often have to pay to access their information. Not ideal when you're on a budget.

WHAT INFORMATION DO YOU WANT TO GATHER?

If you're completely lost and don't even really

understand why you're doing this, let's go over a brief list of things you probably want to know about your target market and the area you're selling to. I'll also add why some of this information can help you.

What are my customer's shopping or buying habits?

What are my customers willing to pay for the goods I'm selling?

The answer to these questions will help you understand what your customer values and how much money they're willing to spend on your goods. You may make the best high-end croissants or bougie donuts around, but if your customer base is a bunch of teens and 20-somethings who don't normally pay high-end prices, you're not going to get anywhere.

How large is my target market?

I've talked about this one in the identifying your target market section, but it bears repeating. It's awesome you want to sell organic gluten free, vegan donuts, but if the only people realistically buying these are a handful of people, you're not going to sell very many.

Who is my competition in my market? In my area?

What are my competitors' weaknesses? What are their strengths?

Knowing what your competition is doing well, and doing poorly, gives you a great advantage. You can reach customers you know your competition is missing out on, and improve on what they door poorly to pull their customers. This sounds harsh, but know that your competition will do the exact same thing with you in order to succeed.

What makes you different from your competition?

Good, detailed research into your competition is going to help you understand how you can stand out, too. This is so important. If you're a carbon copy, accidentally or not, of your competition, you're not giving customers any reason to leave them for your business.

A WEBSITE AND YOUR ONLINE SPACE

Your website is actually a very, very important part of owning a running a business, and honestly? It should be established before you ever really get off the ground. There are a lot of business owners, especially ones who set up locally, who don't seem to think they need one.

You do. You need one.

Once you have your brand and your name down, get a domain that plays into that. GoDaddy and NameCheap are two popular hosting sites where you can buy your domain name and a hosting package. WordPress is easy to set up, and finding a basic theme that works for you is as easy as scrolling through pages of available themes to figure out what you like, and then selecting the best one.

If you don't have any ability or interest in setting up your site, this is something you can outsource to a professional. However... it's not as intimidating as you may think, so I would encourage you to at least consider doing it yourself and saving some cash. After all, the more money you can save in this situation, the more money you can put back into the business later on, in other situations.

Once you have your website established, conventional advice says you should also start a blog. You can talk about your journey with baking, how you develop recipes for your bakery and your life, and what makes you passionate about it.

This... is a little old school, but it can help drive traffic to your website and establish yourself and your brand, so it's not a bad idea. It's up to you if you want to put the time into it, but there are few downsides, other than the time investment of writing about your life and passions.

Note: If you struggle with spelling or grammar, I'm not here to judge you! You're a baker, you might not be a writer. Grammarly is a free plug in for the web or processing programs, like Word, that will not just spell check what you're writing but help you use proper grammar and punctuation to get the best final product. I highly recommend using it.

The reason establishing your presence before you open your business up to the public and start selling your goods is that you have established yourself. You're someone, not just a stranger who put up a website overnight. As soon as you settle on a name, a path, and a brand, start working on your site and establishing that trust.

You can even include baking tips for newbies, or recipes that you're not concerned about sharing. Maybe offering up a sugar cookie recipe that was a few revisions ago, and note that if they want the final, truly perfect version, they can stop into the bakery and pick up a few!

SHOULD I SELL ONLINE?

Yet another great question! If you're an online-only bakery, the answer obviously is yes, you should absolutely sell online, and you're going to need your business to be set up in order to do that properly.

If you're not an online bakery, you need to decide if it's worth it to sell online. There are several things to consider.

Shipping baked goods can be a serious hassle. Serious hassle. Think about the best time to eat a fresh bagel, or a cookie, or a cupcake. Fresh is the keyword, and the longer it sits, the worse it tastes. Even a great cupcake really isn't great if it has been sitting around for a few days.

For that reason, overnight or two-day shipping is probably not a luxury, but a priority. You need to reach out to shippers like UPS, FedEx, and USPS to get accurate quotes on what it would cost to ship a variety of boxes.

Once you get quotes, you're going to need to source packaging material. In line with our discussion on branding, depending on your target market you may want to spring for branded boxes, shipping filler, and more. Finding out how much more it is per package is important. If you are operating an online-only bakery, remember that the unboxing of the product is so much like walking into a bakery for the first time for your customers. You need to create a pleasant, enjoyable experience, and that probably comes with nicer packaging. Just think about how many unboxing videos are online, too!

At this point, it's time to experiment. You should never blind send baked goods, you need to test everything you do.

Package a few cookies, a few cupcakes, or whatever you're planning on baking and selling, and ship them around town. Your parents? Friend from college? Cousins, uncles, nephews?

Send them baked goods! In exchange for some free deliciousness, ask them to tell you when they get their packages, and for pictures of the goods. Consider even writing up a small questionnaire for people you trust, asking them the condition of the baked goods, how they tasted, if they were still fresh and delicious, and more.

You can even ship them to yourself to find out how long it takes and get a quality check.

You may have to adjust your expectations. Shipping may be more for states farther away, or you might need to adjust pricing in general to accommodate extra packing materials. It's important to know this first.

TAKING PAYMENT

If you're going to be selling online, you need to – shocker! – take payment online, too. There are numerous different online platforms that can help.

PayPal is probably one of the most common, though it is considered a little old school anymore. With PayPal, you can create a business account and get a 'buy now' button.

Square is another popular platform that lets a business take payment, and it's popular with both new and more established businesses. Like PayPal, you can simply drop a buy now button on your page and you can take payment and information from customers.

Shopify is the newer person in the market, and they have done a lot of good in the past few years to expand their services and provide what businesses need to take payment, send goods, and grow. Shopify will let you set up a whole store on your website, add items easily, set pricing and shipping, and even take all of the information, including secured payment, from your customers.

I'm not a shill for the company, I swear – but they really fit into the market well, and did something no other company did all in one service.

If you're just starting out and you're a little nervous about setting up a shop and taking payment, Shopify is probably your best bet.

It's secure, your customers can trust putting their credit card information into it, and it is pretty user friendly. You don't have to be an expert with computers or the internet to be able to manage Shopify and your store.

Whatever you choose, whatever direction you take for your online store, you need to be sure you can securely take payment, your shop looks professional, and you have an easy way to manage it. It should never be a struggle to mark an item as out of stock, add new items, or remove seasonal offerings.

SOCIAL MEDIA PRESENCE

The biggest way the game has changed over the years is social media. When I tell you billions of people use social media each and every day, I'm not joking or exaggerating. In 2020, a study from the Pew Research Center noted that about 72% of the public uses some type of social media, from TikTok to Facebook, Instagram, and more. In 2005, that number was just 5%. The biggest demographic is the 18-29 crowd, but 40% of people 65 and older also use social media. There's no age limit to having and maintaining your own Facebook page, after all, which is still the most popular social media platform despite the Gen Z exodus of recent years.

It's very important that you have and maintain social media across a variety of platforms. This is a huge way customers are going to be able to find your products, connect with your brand, and learn more about you as a business.

Let's spend a few minutes talking about good social media practices. Some of these might feel 'obvious' to you – others you may not have thought about, but make sense. Even if you know some of these rules, the refresh is important, so don't skip this part.

A BUSINESS ONLY PAGE ON EACH PLATFORM

You need a separate business page for your bakery business, even if you're still very small and baking out of your kitchen following cottage food laws. I don't want to be rude, but customers don't care about your latest outfit, tattoo, or that your child won the spelling bee. They don't. They want to know about your products, what you offer, and who you are as a business, not a person.

Keep all of your personal achievements or situations just that, personal – on your personal page. Keep your business page all about your business and what you do, not about your personal life. Save the drama for your mama, as they say. (Do kids say that anymore?)

You should maintain a Facebook page at the very least, though I recommend having an Instagram as well. Depending on your sales method and your target market, having these accounts are a great way to connect with your consumers. If you are making trendier items or you want more popularity, TikTok may be a great platform for you as well, though it is a video-only platform. I'll touch on that in a minute.

TWITTER IS IMPORTANT, TOO

Facebook and Instagram get a lot of attention, but Twitter is important, too. It's not as obvious as to how, but sharing Tweets about upcoming events, funny memes, or important announcements are all a good idea.

While this platform isn't as connected as Facebook and Instagram, it should be used regularly. You can post similar information, but be mindful of the character count and image limit – you can share four images, and only 280 characters, including hashtags and emojis.

You should use all the standard posting etiquette on Twitter as you do Facebook or Instagram. Quality pictures, positive content, and relevant content to your business and to selling!

OBVIOUS INFORMATION IS OBVIOUS

After you set up your business pages, be sure that all of the 'important' information is obvious. Your hours, your location (if you have one), and your contact information should be easy to access for anyone looking for more information.

Even if you don't have a physical location, a link to your website, your email address, and a blurb about your business is so important! Make sure that your profile picture is clear and easy to understand, and every time you scan your Facebook business page, it's completely clear who you are and what you're all about.

If you're concerned, check out some of your competitor's Facebook pages. What do you like? What don't you like? Is it hard to see what is going on, or difficult to figure out what they offer or when they're open?

QUALITY PICTURES AND VIDEO

It's important that you take thoughtful, high-quality pictures for your social media pages. This does not mean you have to spend a ton of money on a camera, though, so stop adding that $800 Nikon to your Best Buy online cart.

With the advancements in phones and technology, there's a good chance the phone in your pocket right now is more than enough to get you off the ground.

Lighting is the most important step, but even this can be handled easily. You can get a cheap ring light on Amazon for less than $30, and it's going to up your photo game dramatically. Look for items marketed to social media influencers, as these folks are going to be the ones who most often use this type of item.

Your background is also important, and for this – and the angles you take – look at what is popular online right now. Check out websites like Bon Appetite or popular recipe blogs that share professional-grade images. What is in the background of these photos? How is the picture styled? Good lighting in a clean, neutral location (maybe with pops of colors, like flowers or a fun tablecloth) is probably all you need.

Before you post the picture on your social media feed, though, ask yourself: does this photo look professional, or does it look like a quick photo I would snap for a friend? Does my product look as good as it possibly can? Is it accurately representing the final product, and would I want to buy this product if I just saw the image?

If the answer is yes, you can move on to the next steps, which is what to attach to your post.

No matter if you're promoting a new product, sharing images of products being packaged up and ready to sell, or something else entirely, always include what it is you're posting and information about it, including pricing. While this won't ward off the questions about pricing entirely (we all know some folks choose not to read), it will help curb those questions. Don't just share a photo of a beautiful blueberry donut with no information! Tell your customers exactly what it is, where they can buy it, when they can pick it up, and how much one or a dozen are!

If you're sharing custom creations, like a wedding or birthday cake, you don't need to include the pricing, but the flavor of the cake or more information about it is always helpful. "We got the chance to make this beautiful Dutch double chocolate cake with dark chocolate and raspberry filling for a wedding this weekend. What can we make for your special event?" It doesn't have to be complicated, but it shouldn't be posted by itself!

REMEMBER YOU'RE IN SALES

You're always selling. You and your business are on social media for one thing – to make money. Don't get distracted by anything else, and always focus on the sales aspect. If your posts aren't going to share goodwill or generate income for your business, they shouldn't be shared. Period.

Again, this is one of those things that seems obvious, but really isn't. So many folks do not put this into practice when starting out!

Note: I did not say just sell. Sharing goodwill or attracting attention to your page is awesome! You can share local news or events, especially if you're involved in the events. Sharing content that engages your customers is a great way to keep your name in their minds, and spread cheer. As always, work to keep your social media presence positive and rewarding, not negative.

INTERACT WITH CUSTOMERS

Social media is a very personal experience for most users. While this obviously isn't your personal page (did I drill that into you enough?! I see this mistake ALL the time with new small businesses!), you should be encouraging that personal interaction. Respond to questions on posts right away, or thank them for taking the time to post if someone says it "looks delicious".

Replying to messages on social media is also important. While I personally think that things like texting and social media messages should be handled like email (respond at your earliest convenience, there is no rush), many customers expect relatively quick responses. I check my business social media pages at least twice a day, once in the morning before noon and once in the evening, as the day is winding down. At this point, I'll respond to any messages I get including people asking about prices, availability, and more.

Depending on the day, I'll check social media sporadically, as I get a chance. On some busy days I only check in on scheduled times, while others I'm on several times a day checking up on posts or keeping up conversations.

Social media offers a huge opportunity to connect with your customers and build brand loyalty. You're absolutely leaving money on the table if you're utilizing it fully.

DON'T EVER SAY "PM ME FOR DETAILS"

Customers hate this. Seriously, they despise when a business or user says "PM me for details", "inbox me for prices!", or "send me a message and I can share this with you." If someone asks you for a price or more details and you're not willing to share on the public post for whatever reason, or you need more details, you need to be the one sending them a message. A simple reply could be, "I'm messaging you now with all the details!", and you can follow that up with a personal message from your account to them asking for more details, or going into specifics.

People are so used to instant answers, purchases, and gratification that they do not want to be delayed. Plus, it's sort of rude. They're asking you, don't put the pressure back onto them. You're in sales right now, after all.

SHOULD I USE TIKTOK?

Good question! If you're somehow not familiar, TikTok is a social media platform that has blown up in the past few years, especially with Gen Z-ers. However, you can find many people from many walks of life on the platform.

It is primarily a way to share videos with others. There are trends involving dances, songs, actions, and more. It's a really interactive platform that has over 1 billion people using the app each month. That's... a lot of people, honestly.

While it may not have the same marketing potential at the moment as Facebook and Instagram, it is a great way to get videos of your goods out to people, and grow your audience. Doing fun duets with people who share similar content, sharing in progress videos, and even talking about your new lines of products are all great content.

Be sure to link your TikTok to your other social media platforms, plus your website. Your customers should never struggle to find you on any platform.

Taking good videos for TikTok is just like taking good

photos. Make sure the lighting is good, and your content makes sense. Silly stuff is fine sometimes, but showcasing your goods or your business should be your main focus. People love videos of the baking process, of bread rising, of 'satisfying' decoration, etc.

While it's impossible to say how the future of social media will go, I think we're going to see more and more people utilizing TikTok. There is really no downside to keeping up with a TikTok, as long as you have the time.

HOW OFTEN SHOULD I POST?

This is a question I get a lot from new business owners. How often should I post on social media?

I'm going to tell you it's dependent, on where your time is going, how much you have to do, etc. I encourage at least one post a day, though.

Surprised? Yeah, some folks are – because for many people not running a business page, that seems like a lot. But it's not!

You want to keep your business at the front of folks

minds, and posting regularly helps. You can post product pictures, featured sales or deals you're running, a picture of your front case stocked for the morning... anything in your everyday working life can apply.

It should always be business related, of course. I know I have said this previously, but I can't stress this enough.

If posting each and every day feels overwhelming, you can actually schedule posts out days or even weeks in advance. I like spending some time once a week and scheduling posts out for that week – each Monday morning I do it, and then I don't have to worry about my regular posting schedule. I still sometimes throw in a surprise post or video, but if I don't have time? It's not the end of the world.

CAN I POST TOO MUCH?

Yes! You absolutely can post too much to social media. You don't want your customers or those who follow you to get annoyed by your posts, or see your name at the top of their feed multiple times a day. While social media has algorithms that choose what to show users and when, you still run the risk of simply being over the top.

Just as I recommended once a day at a minimum, I do not recommend posting more than 3 times a day. Of course, there are some exceptions. If you're having an event, you can absolutely post pictures, information, time, even countdowns on your social media feed. If you have important information to share, like you're out of your most popular donut or you have a limited-time special, you can post that in addition to your regular posts.

You're never trying to blow up someone's feed. Be thoughtful with what you post!

USING A SOCIAL MEDIA MANAGEMENT PROGRAM

There are numerous tools to help you schedule posts, including Feedly, CoSchedule, Planable, and Sked Social. Find one that fits in your budget, and that you like using. I like using something called Sprout Social, specifically, which lets my manage all of my social media platforms in one spot, schedule posts in advance, and quickly, easily see what is working for you and what isn't.

For me, that is the biggest thing I look for in a social media manager – I want to be able to immediately know what posts took off and what wasn't popular. I cannot recommend this enough, because it really is the best way to know quickly how to keep the attention of your audience.

USING STORIES

One of the newer functions of Facebook, and a long-time function of Instagram, is the Stories tab. It's almost like a mini TikTok in that you can share short videos, but also images. Users who follow you essentially hit the Stories tab and get automatically shown the next in what can sometimes feel like a never-ending loop of stories from all of the accounts they follow.

If you're not posting stories on these platforms, you are missing out on eyes on your business.

While you shouldn't double post (as in, use the same exact post you shared on your main feed in your stories), you can post similar things. Did you post a picture of your bakery case today? In your stories you can go into more detail, zooming in onto the individual items or even highlighting one. You can also do fun questions, or ask for suggestions on what your viewers want to see next.

Instagram stories let you put interactive buttons that engage your audience.

A good balance of video and pictures is nice, and you're going to want to post pretty regularly to stories. Again, I recommend at least once a day, but you can honestly post 2-3x a day on your stories. You won't be clogging up feeds with unnecessary posts, because people choose to look at stories and can easily skip the ones they don't want to view or interact with.

MARKETING AND ADVERTISING WILL CHANGE YOUR LIFE

I have no doubt that you are so very excited to start your journey and open your doors, literally or metaphorically depending on how you're selling your product. After all, you have spent months, sometimes years, agonizing over the decision to open this business. You have put countless hours and late nights into this business, not even to begin talking about the money you have dumped into it. From starting a website to licensing your business, even just the raw goods to test a recipe a hundred different times to ensure it's not just perfect, but perfectly replicable.

However... your neighborhood and potential customers may not be as excited as you are, and you need to acknowledge that. In fact, unless you have put some serious work into it, the vast majority of potential customers won't even know your business exists.

This is where marketing comes in.

Marketing is vitally important. It's how people know you exist, know what you sell, and become interested in your product. Just blindly opening your doors and hoping for the best is going to get you almost nowhere fast, and be incredibly discouraging.

Marketing is where it's at.

YOU DON'T NEED A MARKETING DEGREE

Just the word marketing or the phrase running ads tends to strike fear into the hearts of new business owners, who know almost nothing about this sort of thing.

I'm here to tell you that you do not need a marketing degree in today's climate to successfully market and run your business. Don't let anyone lie to you and tell you that you do – honestly, the world is changing so fast that folks who got their degree ten years ago may not even know all the best strategies.

I'm here to teach you the basics of marketing your bakery and appealing to your target market. This should include everything you need starting out, and will help you get your business off the ground. At the end of the day, what you put into marketing you're going to get out.

No, I'm not just talking financials, though that is true. It's more than just the money, it is the time and effort, too. Taking the time to craft thoughtful and unique posts, emails, and marketing strategies as a whole will absolutely pay off in the long run.

MARKETING EMAILS: THEY WORK

For the Gen Z-ers reading this, you're going to think this is so old school. But it's in here because it works. Having an email list of past or potential customers, and sending them periodic emails about promotions, new items, or just as a reminder you exist really does work.

Before you fire up your email account and start typing,

though, consider... well, not. Just sending a normal email, even with a few embedded pictures, isn't enough.

Head into your Promotional email folder and see what other companies are doing. Sign up for local or national bakeries that offer an email list, and look at the types of emails they send out.

Mailchimp is probably the most popular email marketing service out there, but there are numerous other platforms that you can go with if you don't like them for some reason. Essentially what you are looking for is a program that lets you input a list of email addresses, and will send out emails to your customers on that list. You can choose what you send and how often, and craft specific templates and designs that align with your brand and are very professional and polished.

At the end of the day, you want your emails to be professional. You're a business, and you're selling a product, you're not emailing your BFF about something.

If you're going to do seasonal or monthly specials or flavors – which I encourage! – be sure to include these in your emails. New store happenings? Include those, too! Include all of the new and exciting things going on in your business right now.

What you shouldn't do is over email. Ensure that you find a balance between keeping your customers updated and absolutely annoying them. Every day is a firm no. Once a week, or once every two weeks, is more standard for an established brand. Don't go months without an update, though – again, we're going for a professional brand. I recommend finding a schedule you can stick to (like every other week), and making it a priority.

LOCAL ADVERTISING

Advertising locally is also smart. Even if you're an online-only business, people like to support local business owners, and it's a great way to drum up new customers.

Flyers are the easiest way to get your name out there. Post flyers at local hot spots with a bulletin board, like libraries, bookstores, and coffee shops. If you don't feel like you can design a professional flyer for your business, you can absolutely hire that out. Fivver or UpWork has tons of professionals interested in helping you promote your business. Look at what other local and national businesses are doing to find examples of formatting and style.

You should also have a good quality business card, and never hesitate to give it out. Your business card should have your bakery name, your hours if applicable, and contact information, like your location, your website, and your phone number. If you're selling anything specialized, like keto-friendly foods or hard-to-find items, adding that might be a good idea.

You can easily design and order professional business cards online, and they are not as expensive as you might expect. Take the time to design a professional one and it will be worth your time.

If you have a physical location, hosting community events is an amazing way to get the community involved in your bakery. Fundraisers, community events, and get-togethers are all good ideas. Contact your local activists or community leaders and find out how you can help. Schools and local clubs are always looking for quality partners.

Don't hesitate to join in on local events, too, instead of just hosting. Is there a local baking competition, food show, or even an artisan and local vendor fair? Get in there and share your stuff, especially as you are first starting out. Look for any and every opportunity to not just interact with your community, but put your food in their hands. If what you're selling is great, they will be back.

The best local advertising you can do, however, is just be friendly. Customer service is so important. I have spent many years of my life catering to the public, and I will never agree with the term "the customer is always right", because that is just absurd. Instead, I buy into the term "the customer is king", a term I first read in regards to the Chinese way of handling customers. Your customer may not always be right, but they are the ones keeping your lights on.

Treat them as such. Never allow customers to degrade or berate your staff, of course, but small issues that are easy to fix? Those can be taken care of without too much stress or hassle. Ask yourself when you feel yourself getting frustrated or upset – is this the hill you want to die on? An unhappy customer is far more likely to complain online than a happy customer.

I've seen many, many small businesses make this mistake. It's hard to not feel incredibly protective of your business. It's almost like having a baby – you have grown this small business from just a small idea in the back of your head. You've struggled and fought, had late nights and early mornings, put your literal blood, sweat, and tears into it. Someone coming in and being rude to your, your staff, or giving you a hard time can feel like a personal attack.

It's not, so you need to remember that first. Be patient, remember your customers keep your lights on, and take care of issues within reason how you would want them taken care of if the roles were reversed. An unhappy customer is far more likely to leave a negative review or share their negative experience than a happy customer. Always remember this.

There's no use in being right if you end up losing your business due to bad publicity.

REACH OUT TO THE LOCAL NEWS

If you're starting a local bakery, be sure to contact your local newspaper! Everyone loves a feel-good story, and it is literally free press for you. Think about what you want prospective customers to know about you. Are you a life-long local looking to make a difference in your community? Do you want to share a story about why baking is your passion?

Make it compelling, and consider offering samples to local press professionals, too, so they can write and share their own experiences with your bakery.

LOCAL ADS WORK, TOO... BUT BE SMART

Sometimes a local ad can bring in a ton of new customers, especially if you pair it with a seasonal or new item. "Check out X at the bakery", or "Bring in mom to try out the new Mother's Day special"... whatever you're running.

However, you need to be smart about it. I've given this advice without thinking about it, and realized not everyone reads their local newspapers as my area does. Is your paper popular? Does it sell well? Who reads it, and who might see the ad? How long will it run, and how much will it cost to run? I've seen it cost as little as $20 and as expensive as over $1,000, which is absurd. Use your common sense, and don't run a local ad if no one reads your local news or they're charging more than you can afford.

NETWORKING MATTERS

No matter if you're a local in-person bakery or an online-only bakery experience, local networking matters. Reach out to local experts and professionals in your area, like event planners, caterers, and even florists. Wedding venues often keep a list of related vendors - see if you can get on that list. When I got married (an embarrassingly long time ago), our venue offered a double-sided sheet with the names and contact information of local bakeries, DJs, photographers, and more. Everything we might need as a starting point.

Check out local groups, too. Donating a few dozen cookies to the Rotary Club, a local non-profit organization, or any local gathering and group might be an upfront cost, but it's free feel-good local publicity! Don't hesitate to target local organizations that may have influential people within them that would want to hire you for other events. It's all about getting your name out there.

In my experience, realtors are also an underserved professional corner for bakers. Many realtors I partner with now simply don't get a lot of inquiries, which surprises me. Realtors are always going to or hosting events, having open houses, and more. Fresh, local cookies are a hit at an open house, and do a lot to make potential buyers more comfortable. Reach out to see what sort of deal you can strike up with the local community.

ADVERTISING ONLINE

This is the bread and butter for most businesses. More and more, people rely on the internet for all of their needs, and it's not unusual for a customer to find out about a new business or product from the internet.

Social media is going to be your biggest marketing source, for the most part. We have already talked about setting up your social media accounts, but if you haven't done so yet, or you're putting it off, I suggest you get to it!

Facebook and Instagram both allow you to 'boost' posts, their main form of advertisements. When you're scrolling through your own personal social media feeds and you see a 'Sponsored' post, that is what these are! You, too, can show up in someone's Facebook or Instagram feed.

It is very simple, which is great. You can choose a post that you think will do well, tell the platform how much money you want to spend promoting it, and who you want to see it. Think 20-somethings local to your area are your target demographic? Create a post that you believe will appeal to them, choose how long the post will run and be sponsored, pick those folks as your demographic, and watch your views go up.

It's really that simple. The longer you do this, the better idea you'll get of what posts do well and what isn't engaging. Again, if you aren't quite sure where to start, check out the posts from local bakeries. What posts do they promote? What posts in the last few months have gotten the most attention? I would never, ever tell you to copy directly what they are doing, but seeing what is working for your competition and how you can make that work for you is never wrong.

This might seem like a lot of effort, I understand, but putting in the work now is not just going to save you from dealing with unsuccessful posts, and in the long term will not only save you money, but gain you sales and customers.

You should always promote your best, most relevant posts. If you're creating a seasonal line, for example, start posting about it as soon as you introduce the product and promote that. Don't choose older posts, posts with poor images, or bare posts to promote. The other day I was on my own personal Facebook (this is a true story), and I saw the most confusing sponsored post. It was just two lines of text, no images or pictures, saying that a local building was a 'great' retail location to buy 'local goods'.

The post didn't include pictures of the local goods. There was no indication of what local businesses were a part of the retail building, and it didn't even have an address or website so I could easily find that information. Someone paid for that post!

Don't make that mistake.

Instagram and Facebook are both owned by the same company, which you may or may not know. Facebook picked up Instagram quite a while ago, and has integrated to each other quite well. You can cross-post to both platforms with ease, and managing your promotions is easy, too.

You should be able to see your promotions and posts

from one page, and both platforms offer statistics and analytic information. You can easily and quickly tell which posts are successful, and what isn't being engaged with. You should also be able to see when people are seeing and interacting with your posts. Maybe your customers mostly use Instagram in the early mornings, before work, and in the evenings, after their commute. You want to focus your posting during these times, so they are more likely to see and interact with you.

This really is a trial and error process. You're not going to be getting tens of thousands of likes or comments immediately, and it's a slow and steady process to build up your following and get people engaged. This time is well spent, though – according to Instagram's business information, 90% of people who are on the platform follow at least one business account, and 2 in 3 of the users surveyed say that Instagram enables them to interact with a brand when they otherwise wouldn't be able to. 130 million users engaged with shopping content each month.

Even more surprising, a staggering 50% of users surveyed say they are more interested in a brand after seeing an ad for the brand on the platform. Instagram has done a really excellent job seamlessly integrating advertisements and promotions into users' feeds. This is huge, and gaining this sort of trust and interest with your community can really benefit you in the long run.

I mentioned in a previous section that the photos you put on social media are important, and I'm just going to expand on that for a moment. The photos and videos you post are important. For many potential customers, this is the only exposure they're going to get to your product before they purchase it... or close your social media and dismiss you.

Once again, if you are completely lost on what makes a good picture or post good, look at what other bakeries are doing and what looks good to you. Ask yourself if the photo looks polished and professional, if it makes you want that item, etc.

If you don't feel like you're getting the right results, try to figure out why. Does your photo look different because it's darker, with worse lighting? Try to take your pictures in natural light, or use a ring light for social media. Does it look flat? Make sure your phone is in Portrait mode if it has one, and adjust the angles that you're taking the picture to get not just the best 'side' of the item, but the most flattering final product.

Once you get a system that works for you, it will be a lot easier, but the pictures you post and share are so important.

Since TikTok has taken over, short videos are becoming more and more popular. Even if you aren't on the platform (though it's free to sign up, and basically free advertising for you!), using video is a great way to keep a customer on your page longer and hold their attention.

You can do videos of your final product, fast-forward in progress videos of baking, assembling, or even decorating. Are there any trends you can jump on with your bakery to appeal to a younger crowd? Even if it seems 'silly', videos like decoration progress or bread rising usually are very popular!

At the time of writing, Instagram is looking to directly compete with TikTok by promoting more videos in user feeds. This means that you if you use Instagram regularly for your business, posting videos is going to do nothing but help you. I think it's only going to continue to be a focus in the coming years, so don't neglect this very important aspect.

Posting in your local community groups is such a good way to get local attention, and bring people to your business. When I was just starting out, groups like these didn't really exist – but in the last 8 or 10 years, and even more recently, they have really taken off.

Search Facebook for community groups in your area. Personally, I'm part of two 'food-centric' groups for my local area, plus two 'discussion' pages. Residents post about new restaurants, specials, a great meal they had, and in the discussion pages they talk about new happenings in the neighborhood, local sports, construction... you get the point.

Sharing your posts about new specials, seasonal offerings, or even just a short promo post about what you have going on today is a great way to get eyes on your business and people through your door. I've seen these local communities really come together to support the small businesses around them, and push businesses deserving of it to new levels of success.

You're absolutely missing out if you're not using these pages. As always, though, be sure to read the rules to know promotion is allowed, and be smart about it. You probably don't want to blow up a group with posts every single day, especially if you live in a smaller community with a smaller page!

Google Ads are another way you can reach your customers and gain new viewers. Instead of focusing on a target market, though, like Instagram or Facebook, you focus on keywords. You can, for example, set it up so that anytime anyone searches "bakeries in x town", your name pops up. Maybe you have a specialty, like gluten free croissants. You can pay Google to show your bakery when someone searches for that phrase.

Google Ads are old school, but they are still around because they do work. People trust what Google has to offer them, and most don't even really realize how the ad system works. They don't even notice they're clicking on a sponsored post!

These are also very easy to run. You decide what keyword you want, how long you want to pay for that keyword, and what the ad says. Be sure to always use proper grammar and spelling (a surprisingly overlooked issue!), and consider the page the ad will direct to.

If you're advertising gluten free croissants to be shipped to their door, don't direct the ad to a page about cookies or cakes. Nine times out of 10, your customer will click off instead of digging through the site for what they are looking for.

COUPONS WORK

If you're struggling driving traffic into your business, or you're looking to attract new customers, a coupon can be a great idea. Don't ever give away what you can't afford, but a "buy eleven and get the twelfth free" cookie deal might bring a dozen new people into your store. You could be creating repeat customers – and potentially getting more sales. They may pick up a cupcake or muffin with their cookies, or get a coffee or tea.

Offering online-only or social media exclusive specials can also work really well. I've had great luck with posting on social media in the morning offering a free cookie or coffee to the first 20 people to say a specific phrase to the cashier. Someone sees that and goes, wow, I wanted to get coffee anyway. Might as well go in, get a muffin, a cup of coffee... it works.

You can run coupons in your local paper, offer up coupons or discount codes for people who sign up for your email newsletter, and even offer coupons to first-time visitors at your store. If you have a physical location, doing punch cards for cookies or coffee is a great way to build local loyalty and have people coming in again and again.

NEVER STOP MARKETING

I can't stress this enough – never stop marketing. Even if you feel like you're in a fine position right now, it's important to keep pushing and growing. Unless you're at a point where you literally cannot sustain any more growth, you should always have your marketing going.

Regular clientele and loyal customers are absolutely a core of a successful business, but people come and go. Circumstances change, and loyalty wanes. You want to make sure you're always bringing in new folks.

It's also likely that someone won't buy from the very first ad they see. Studies suggest that customers may need to hear a name or read about a food place at least three times before they jump in and try it. I'm not entirely sure I buy that, personally, but the more presence you have in the community and online, the more likely people will recognize your brand and want to try you.

For the most part, keep pushing, keep making connections, and keep running marketing, even if it's only a little. It's going to really pay off for you in the long run.

FOOD SAFETY AND RECIPE SECRETS

Food safety matters.

Let me repeat that again – food safety matters. When someone purchases your product to consume, they are putting something you have handled into their mouths, into their bodies, and trusting that you have taken all the necessary precautions to ensure a safe food experience. You know the old saying, you are what you eat? I don't necessarily buy that – I would have been about 80% sugar and 18% fast food in the first few years of building my business if that were the case.

However, more than many other businesses you could start, handling food can be scary. You need to make sure that you are respecting people, taking care to follow proper food safety procedures, and being smart about what you put into your baked goods and how you are sharing that with your customers.

LABELING: IT MATTERS

I've got a very un-funny story to share with you, only tangentially related but I think it's important. This was told to me by a friend, who worked in a restaurant during college. It's one of those memories that will always stick with her, and she shared it with me when we were talking about my journey into baking. The restaurant menu, like most menus, did not have allergens listed.

There was one particular table seated in the section next to hers. The server had been with the company longer than she had, but was a little lazy. The table was a teenage girl and her parents traveling through the area.

They asked, does the apple crisp have nuts? The server

says no, absolutely not. The father reiterates, are you sure? Because she has an allergy. The server says absolutely not, there are no nuts.

I'm sure you can see where this is going. The server didn't tell anyone about the allergy, the apple crisp absolutely did have nuts in the topping, and the server lost his job. Luckily for the family, the local hospital was only a few blocks away, and the manager on duty ended up driving the family himself to the hospital and sitting in the lobby for over 7 hours, until the girl was cleared before driving them back to their car.

That server almost killed a girl because he couldn't be bothered to read a label or ask someone. While this situation will probably never happen exactly like this in your own bakery, it's so very, very important to offer comprehensive, detailed labeling on your packages and online. Allergies exist, they are terrifying for those struggling with them, and you have a responsibility as someone who bakes professionally (which is what you are doing, now that you're starting a business) to help prevent accidents just like this.

I'm going to help walk you through some ways to avoid

literally harming people, and also maintaining good food safety practices. I'm not being dramatic when I say it's a matter of life or death.

RECIPES MATTER

When we bake for ourselves, I find that each time we make a recipe, it's a little different. Before I started baking professionally, I never measured vanilla extract. Much like garlic in a savory application, I let my heart tell me how much extract I needed, not any recipe. However, that doesn't fly when you're baking professionally.

There are two reasons. The first should be obvious: a person is expecting a specific product. When you follow a set recipe each and every time, the end result is always the same. No matter how many batches of sugar cookies you're making over the course of days or weeks, they always taste the same. Someone might come in Monday and love that cookie – when they come in again on Friday, that cookie should taste the same.

The less obvious reason is, yep, allergies. If you only sometimes add almond flour to your muffin recipe (do not recommend, by the way), you can't give anyone an accurate ingredient list. If you add both almond extract and vanilla extract to your buttercream sometimes, but not always, you may accidentally trigger an allergic reaction in someone who has previously consumed a food and never had a reaction.

Allergies are weird. I knew a woman who couldn't eat raw tomato. Seriously, a slice of tomato made her sick, but if it was cooked it was fine. No one believed her when she tried to order a burger in a restaurant, and salads could be a nightmare.

When you're crafting recipes for your bakery, always measure your ingredients and always write down those measurements. Once you have a final product you like, you need to follow that recipe always. If you change the recipe, I recommend putting it on the packaging or in the signage. "New, improved recipe!", or something along those lines. Always let people know.

PROPER LABELING

Depending on the state you're in, legal requirements for labels may vary. As always, you should adhere to your state requirements for food labeling, as well as any FDA requirements. I know in many counties and states, restaurants or bakeries are required to put the caloric count of the food they're selling. This is a bummer (no one wants to know how many calories are in a slice of cheesecake, let's be honest), and you may have to take your recipes and final products to a nutritionist or food expert in order to get accurate numbers.

I put an ingredient list on every single item I ship out, as well as listing them on my website. I do this not so that people can 'steal my secrets', but so that I can help include those who have allergies and keep everyone safe. I have a list of ingredients available at my in-person locations behind the counter that my staff can access, but I don't necessarily offer them to each and every customer. I just don't think it's necessary, but I do have it available if it's needed.

At the very minimum, I encourage you to include any major allergens in your packaging and labeling, regardless on if you're required by law or not. It's honestly just a good thing to do to help your fellow human beings, and ensure everyone is safe and sound.

PROPER CLEANING

Cleaning your business is vital. Again, I touched on this briefly before, but maintaining a clean and safe working environment is essential if you not just want to be successful, but even just stay in business.

Have a strict cleaning schedule, and stick to it. There are some things, like mopping the floors, wiping down counters, and cleaning dishes or equipment that must be done each and every day. However, deep cleans of stovetops, fridges, behind equipment, etc., should be done on a rotating schedule. Every Monday, for example, there should be a handful of extra cleaning tasks.

Just a tip I've found that works for my businesses is to not include extra deep cleaning on the weekends, or busy days in general. No one wants to work a crazy business Saturday afternoon, just to have to scrub down the fridge after. When I first started my business I insisted on a spotless kitchen, and scheduled intense cleaning each day.

I still insist on a spotless kitchen, don't get me wrong – but I know if detailed cleaning is scheduled after an exceptionally busy shift, it's just not going to happen.

As mentioned, schedules really do work.

When you first start out, I recommend that you write out a schedule on a daily, weekly, and monthly basis. Open up your scheduling tool of choice – Google has their own calendar, but so does Outlook, and Apple. I like having something that pushes notifications each day to my phone, so I always know what I have to get done, but find something that works for you and your daily life.

Take a sheet of paper and make a list of everything that needs to be cleaned daily. Then, weekly, as in once a week. Next, every other week, and finally, once a month. Schedule these out each day, until every single task has an assigned day. I like using the reoccurring event schedule for these tasks, so I don't have to individually write every Monday task once a week.

Print it out when you've written up your monthly schedule, and post it somewhere you, and any employees you might have, can see it. You can even generate a daily checklist from this monthly calendar, and mark each item off each day. Bonus points if you laminate each day, so you can wipe it clean each evening and reuse next week.

CROSS CONTAMINATION

In the vein of allergens, let's touch on what cross contamination means.

If someone is allergic to peanuts, you obviously can't serve them a chocolate chip cookie with peanut butter in it. However, you also probably can't promise their cookie is completely nut free if you haven't sanitized every single piece of equipment in the kitchen between making a peanut butter cookie and a chocolate chip cookie.

It's important that when you're baking multiple recipes, especially with allergens, you take cross contamination very seriously. Always change your gloves after finishing one recipe and starting another, or handling different batches of things. Be sure to sanitize equipment like mixing bowls, dough hooks, and even work stations between recipes.

Always be honest when someone asks if there is risk of cross contamination as well. If someone has a nut allergy and you've never baked with nuts in your kitchen, let them know that. However, if you know you baked those cookies the same day or even on the same trays, you need to let them know there is a risk of cross contamination.

It's not just about allergens, though. Keep eggshells away from the dough – much of the bacteria in an egg is carried on the shell. Anything with raw egg or flour should be kept away from cooling racks and baked goods. Never let dough rise or raw cookie dough come up to temperature in the area that you have finished products cooling. Never prepare raw dough near finished, baked goods.

Keep everything, and everyone, safe and separate.

CLOTHING AND BAKING SAFETY

I've got long hair. I have had long hair for most of my life, and it's something I like. When I bake at my bakeries, however, it gets pulled back completely and then a hair net goes on. At home, I skip the hair net, because I'm only baking for myself – but the hair still goes back.

It's important to lay down ground rules of clothing and hair expectations, and follow them. This is exceptionally important when you have staff, too.

I require closed toed shoes and long pants in my own bakery, for my baker's safety. Hair must be pulled back neatly, and a hair net is worn. Anything other than short, cropped facial hair is discouraged, and if it's too long, a beard net is worn. Yes, a beard net – like a hair net, but for your face. Bakers are only allowed to wear low profile rings, nothing bulky, and no dangling earrings, necklaces, or bracelets. I wear a silicone wedding band when I bake, and I encourage others to do the same.

This isn't just for the safety of my staff, but for the cleanliness of my kitchen and to ensure there are no surprises baked into my goods. No one wants to find a hair in their cupcakes.

BAKING MATTERS

We have all snuck a spoon of cookie dough before putting it into the oven. We've all tasted raw cake batter to double check that all of the ingredients are in it. It happens, and when you do that, you take the risk of maybe getting sick.

A fun fact is that you're a lot more likely to get ill from consuming raw flour than you are from raw egg... but that doesn't mean raw dough is safe to consume.

It's important to always bake your products thoroughly. If you're going to be creating something like an edible cookie dough to sell, it must be safe to consume. The flour must be baked thoroughly in the oven first, and eggs should not be included. Even with something like lava cakes, you need to be extra careful to ensure that the inside of the product is hot enough to kill any bacteria.

Sound obvious? You would be shocked at how many times I've seen this happen.

ONLY USE YOUR OWN RECIPES

Your recipes are your own – you should never be baking with someone else's, of course. The ethics of using another chef's recipes are... fuzzy, at best. Let's be honest, if you're a professional pastry chef that has worked in professional kitchens for any amount of time, you've picked up a lot of recipes, tips, and tricks along the way.

However... those aren't yours. Where does the line between using a trick or 'hack' you picked up in another kitchen and pulling a whole recipe from their menu lay?

It's fuzzy.

A good rule of thumb is that if you haven't changed the recipe you're using from the original source, it's not your recipe, so don't use it. Developing and creating new recipes takes time, and is a very long process, even for professional chefs. I'm not going to go into all the details on how to create your own recipe, because again, that could fill a whole other book. However, I will help you on the path. This will probably only apply to us home chefs and those without a culinary degree, but I could be wrong!

Let's say you want to make sugar cookies in your bakery, and you need to develop the best sugar cookie recipe to sell to your customers. Your first step should be to do some research. Search online and dig through your recipe books. Is there a standard flour/sugar/egg ratio that you can find? Get yourself the rough proportions of what other, established recipes have.

Once you do that, write down a baseline "recipe" you're going to try, using what you have found from numerous other successful recipes. Maybe you want to add some of your own flavor in, like orange zest or coconut oil, and that's fun! Be sure to start slow, though.

With that baseline recipe, it's time to head to the kitchen. Measure out your ingredients and get baking. If you find that your dough is too, say, dry, or too wet, you can add things to fix that – but always record what you change, so you can replicate it. You never want to modify a recipe and not record those changes, because I promise you, you'll never always remember the exact quantities you used, and there will forever be that once recipe you can't recreate.

Not that I'm speaking from experience, of course. I'll figure you out someday, chocolate orange tart...

I keep a notebook in the kitchen with me, and jot down notable things, like if I changed the order of ingredients that I added, if I put an extra teaspoon of vanilla, if I used more flour, etc. At the end of the recipe, after it's baked and tested, I write a "new" baseline recipe with the changes I made. Then, if it's not perfect, I go back and change things again.

You are not going to hit the nail on the head the first time you try a recipe. That's totally fine, and it's part of making your own recipe and perfecting things. Keep trying, keep pushing. Change little things, and expect to make a recipe a dozen or more times before you really get that perfect result.

KEEPING YOUR RECIPES A SECRET

I talked previously about putting your ingredients on your packaging, and online. This is different from giving away your recipes. A list of raw ingredients, like flour, sugar, egg, and chocolate, is not telling the consumer how much of each is going into a recipe, or what order to mix things, or even what temperature to bake them at.

You probably work pretty hard on all your recipes, and it's going to be priority one in your mind to keep them secret. As mentioned in the section on hiring and training new employees, you are going to want everyone involved in the recipe process to sign a non-disclosure agreement so they cannot share their recipes with others.

In addition, be sure to keep your recipes safe. As basic practice, I have a binder with all the recipes. This book comes out at the start of the day, and each recipe is pulled out and baked. My sheets are laminated, making them perfect for the kitchen environment. You can also use something like an iPad, if you prefer having everything digital as well.

Once we're done baking, all the recipes get gathered back together and put into the binder, which stays locked in the back office. You can also lock the iPad, or otherwise secure your recipes.

I don't recommend hanging them in full view of customers or even visitors to your kitchen, and take care to not allow staff to take pictures of recipes or record them. Honestly? If you have loyal staff that do the same job day in and day out, they'll probably memorize most of the recipe just from use, and that's okay. Don't, however, go out of your way to share your recipes with other people.

Honestly? The risk of someone stealing your recipe for their own bakery is pretty slim. Unless you're creating the most amazing and unique recipes of all time, with crazy off the wall ingredients that are somehow magical and cure all illnesses... you're probably safe. Even famous chefs share recipes occasionally – after all, you can find Christina Tosi's recipes online, or in her cookbooks. The actual recipes that she uses in her bakery.

WHEN TO HIRE EMPLOYEES

You may end up at a point in your bakery business where you need to hire an extra set of hands. Depending on how you're building your business and how fast your business is growing, this could come sooner than you may be expecting.

Hiring can be a big moment for some business owners. Sometimes it's not going to feel real – like, you're really running and growing a successful business – until you hire someone else, and they are reliant on you and your business.

Hiring is a big deal. Let's look at when to hire, how to hire, and I'm going to briefly touch on how to manage. A shocking number of business owners don't seem to understand the difference between owner and manager, and how to treat their employees.

WHEN TO KNOW IT'S TIME

How do you know when it's time hire another employee?

This is going to depend on your type of business. If you're opening a static, traditional bakery location, there's a good chance you're going to need to hire someone right off the bat because running a successful business and doing it all by yourself in this setting is nearly impossible.

However, if you have a less traditional bakery business, like a food truck, a home bakery, or even a takeout only bakery, you may get away with just yourself for a while.

At a certain point you need to ask yourself a series of questions:

Do you feel that your business would benefit from a

second set of hands?

Are your sales limited not necessarily by your customers, but by your production?

Would having another person working in some aspect of your business allow you to grow your business faster?

Can your business financially support a living wage for another human?

If the answer is yes to all of these, then it may be time to reach out to your community and find a willing set of hands to help you grow your business.

FINANCIAL COMMITMENT

It's super serious when you hire someone else. As a business owner, you're going to be used to perhaps not making a salary at first, or not much of one. There may be some months, especially in the beginning, that you're not really taking money for yourself. This is just a fact of owning a business. It's not the fun part, but it's realistic.

However, when you hire someone else, you cannot do that. I have heard horror stories from people who went to work for a small business and struggled to get paid, record their wages properly, and more, all because the business owner couldn't manage their money properly.

For some of you reading this, it will seem so obvious you won't believe I have to say it, but you cannot mess with someone else's livelihood like this. If you agree to pay someone a set rate hourly, you must honor that commitment always, no matter how good or bad the month has been for your business. If you cannot, then your business cannot financially handle another employee, and you need to reevaluate.

Make sense? Okay, good. Now we can move on.

HOW TO FIND EMPLOYEES

Many businesses struggle to find competent, reliable employees. At the time of writing, the US job market is at a point we have never really experienced before, where employers just like you are struggling to find help. Some companies are literally offering to match or best hourly pay from other employers just to have enough staff to open.

I'm not saying this to be discouraging. You can absolutely find good employees! It may be slightly more work than it was a few years ago, but that's okay.

Place ads in places that your prospective employees would go to. If you're near a local college, advertising at the school on bulletin boards or in college newspapers is a good idea. Your local newspaper should have a section to find employees, and you should post there, too. I know most people don't read the newspaper, but there are often online versions of the classifieds, too. At least, my local paper does!

Online resources like Craigslist and Indeed are also great options. People still use these sites to find jobs, so don't discount them!

You can also ask around. Have friends or relatives? Ask them if they know someone looking for a job, especially someone with bakery or retail experience. Reach out to your community and use your connections!

THE ETHICS OF POACHING

There are a lot of articles online or discussions in

forums about the ethics of poaching an employee from another competing shop. I've seen some incredibly questionable advice go around the internet, and both extremes have been represented, so I'm going to give you my opinion of the practice.

You should never poach in a way that is so obvious the entire store knows what you're doing. I would never, ever recommend you going into a bakery or coffee shop with the intent to take an employee away. That's rude, inconsiderate, and intentionally harmful.

If you go to a bakery or coffee shop and get amazing service, or you feel that the person really has a great personality or aura about them, discretely giving the employee your business card after introducing yourself is the best way to do it.

Never announce yourself, be over the top, or downright obnoxious about it. You should never go into an establishment with the intent to poach an employee. The community is small, and you're not doing yourself any favors.

APPLICATION INFORMATION

When taking applications, you need to ask prospective employees to fill out an application. You can find a generic form easily online, but it's important you include information that is relevant to you.

Ask about not only retail experience, but baking or café experience. What previous jobs have they had? How do they interact with customers?

When asking for references you should try to avoid personal references, and instead ask for professional references. Depending on the job you're hiring for, you may end up with applicants who are looking for their first job. That is totally fine, and you should never discount someone without work experience, especially for an entry level job. Try to see if they can provide references from teachers, coaches, or other structured setting.

INTERVIEWING

Conducting a proper interview is so very important. You need to make sure that the person sitting across from you is a good fit, and work well with you, your business, and do well with your customers.

You're more than welcome to meet in your bakery to conduct the interview, but if you're working from a commercial kitchen or your home kitchen, you're probably going to want to conduct your first interview at a neutral location. A library, local coffee shop, or even the food court of a local mall are all options. Explain that you aren't willing to first interview within a kitchen setting.

You should be asking questions that pertain to their work experience, and what they will bring to the table. How do they handle customers? Do they work well under pressure? What job in their past was most like the role they applied for, and did something in particular attract them to the listing?

Avoiding asking the question that every single interviewer asks, "Why do you want to work here?" Look, there's a chance this person applied because they love baking, or love your bakery (if you're established), or want to break into the industry... but if you're looking for a basic cashier or retail person, there is also a better chance that they aren't passionate about baking as much as passionate about paying their bills.

Does this mean they won't be a great employee? Of course not. If they have wonderful customer service skills and attention to detail, they may be your best employee. Just be realistic!

Consider offering 'fake' situations, such as they are forced to deal with a difficult customer or they have to choose between two different choices. Ask what is the right decision in that situation, and then explore why they chose that. You can learn a lot by presenting this sort of situation to a potential hire.

LAY OUT ALL EXPECTATIONS EARLY

It's important before you hire someone to lay out all of the expectations of a potential employee. As a small business, your employees may have to wear a lot of hats – sometimes baking, sometimes talking to customers, serving coffee, packaging orders… it's probably a lot, honestly. That's why laying out your expectations early is so important.

Is there a dress code? Even if you don't have a uniform, like some traditional bakeries might, you probably have an idea about how you'd ideally like your employees to dress. Closed toed shoes, hair back and neat, etc. If you want your employees to wear a branded shirt, it's important you supply them with an appropriate amount for work! It's not just the law in some states, it's what a good employer does, honestly.

Think about what else your ideal employee does. Do they show up on time each day? Probably – lay out an expectation. If they have an emergency, by what time should they call out? An hour before their shift? Three hours? If and when they answer the phone, how should they answer it?

I recommend you writing down all your expectations and allowing a new or prospective employee to read over and agree to them. At the very least, it should be an honesty discussion.

If you're asking something that others may consider unreasonable, I highly recommend you consulting with an employment lawyer for your state. A lot of small businesses get a bad reputation for being an awful employer and asking far too much of their staff. Don't do this. Don't be that guy.

When you're bringing a new employee on board, you will probably want them to sign a non-disclosure agreement. This basically says that they are not permitted to share any trade secrets they learn working for you, including recipes. This is pretty important, even if you're not hiring someone to work in the kitchen with you. Protecting your business should be number one.

Some people recommend employees signing something called a non-compete, too. This is a form that states that if an employee leaves the business (either fired or quit, it doesn't matter) they cannot work for a similar, competing business or start a similar business in a set time frame. The time frame varies, and can be anywhere from a few months to a few years.

I'm going to be honest with you: in my experience, a non-compete really isn't enforceable, and you'd end up spending a lot of money trying to enforce it. You can absolutely have your employees sign one if it makes you feel better, but at the end of the day it's not going to stop them. It's also unreasonable at best to ask your hourly employee who handles phones and packaging to not find a similar job if it doesn't work out with you for whatever reason.

I do have all my own employees sign a non-compete, but it really is there to prevent people from taking what they learned in my own bakery and starting their own, directly competing with me. I would never consider attempting to enforce it with an hourly employee just trying to make it by.

You can get both of these online. Legal Zoom is legitimately an awesome resource where you can actually get real, legal documents that apply to you – I'm not a sponsor, just a big fan. You can also consult a local employment attorney that works within your state if you would feel more comfortable.

HAVE POLICIES, AND ABIDE BY THEM

Think about all of the employers you have had previous to opening your own business. From your very first job in fast food or retail, to any kitchens you have worked in, legal offices... whatever. I'm going to guess that most of those jobs had policies, rules, and regulations.

Things like dress code, as mentioned above, but also like sick policies, call out policies, expectations for language, and more. You should absolutely write all this down and put it together in an employee handbook, and give a copy of the handbook to each and every person you hire.

This is more than just the discussion you have during the interview process with a prospective employee about expectations. These are hard and fast policies, and you should abide by them, with reasonable consequences. Don't fire someone for calling out once, of course, but don't let someone call out each and every week without any repercussions.

Once you have expectations and policies laid out, when someone doesn't follow them, you need to decide what kind of boss you're going to be. I recommend flexible, but firm – however, I can't tell you what type of management style works for you.

I offer my staff several verbal warnings first, depending on what policy or expectation they have failed. If a baker shows up wearing flipflops on Monday, they get sent home to change or simply sent home, if they refuse to come back. The second one results in a written warning, just a note in their file. If they're willing to swap shoes, I let it slide with just a verbal warning.

If it happens next week, I write it down. I will continue to escalate these sort of issues until several written warnings are on file. Having a paper trail to follow a problem employee is so important if you have to terminate them.

If you do not formally record issues you have with an employee, you can be on the hook for unemployment at the very least, and potentially face a lawsuit for unlawful firing depending on your state and local labor laws. This really is not something a small business wants to deal with, or can even financially handle. Don't let it happen to you – be smart. Lay out policies, follow those policies, and formally record any issues.

SELECTIVELY ENFORCING

One side note I'm going to point out is an issue new owners or managers have with selectively enforcing policies or rules. At the end of the day, it's your business, your employees, and you do what you want. However, when you only selectively enforce or punish staff, you're setting a very dangerous precedent.

A lot of new owners struggle with this. They get attached to their staff, they let things slide, but someone they don't particularly like or enjoy in the long run comes in, and that person starts being held to a different standard.

It's not fair. It's not nice. It's not professional. And most of all, it creates a really negative and toxic work environment, fostering negative attitudes, and it will rub off on your customers. A really good employee, who cares about you and your business, won't ask you to bend the rules for them. They'll follow them because they respect you and your business.

Remember that.

DEALING WITH PAYROLL

I've mentioned before that paying your employees is important. That... sounds obvious, but again, I've run into so many questionable business owners who don't seem to realize that.

Paying your employees is important, and having a reliable way to track their hours and conduct payroll is important!

All of your employees should fill out a W-4 form, which will let you legally pay them and report their earnings to the IRS.

Your pay periods should coordinate with the IRS tax withholdings as well, and you can get all that information on the IRS website, unsurprisingly – their Employer's Tax Guide (https://www.irs.gov/publications/p15) is incredibly comprehensive, and will help you understand how to withhold taxes so everything is legal. This is one of those things that is really important. I cannot stress enough how much the IRS does not appreciate not getting the money they are owed.

As far as payroll goes, you have a few options. You can handle it all in-house, or you can contract it out. For many businesses, contracting it out is well worth the money. There are numerous different companies that will help you handle payroll, including ADP, OnPay, and Paychex. Paychex is more expensive, but it also offers HR support and benefit plans, which may appeal to you.

I personally like OnPay, as they use a time tracking software (great for keeping track of your employees hours), set up state and federal tax filings and withholdings, and even has some accounting software. There's also tools to track PTO, documentation, and HR issues.

Patriot is the cheapest option I've found, and if you're looking to run payroll on a budget, this is great. It also integrates with Quickbooks, a very popular bookkeeping tool with small businesses that I also recommend. Pay attention, though – their basic plan doesn't cover state or federal taxes.

Finally, my third recommendation is Square. If you're already using Square for a POS system like many small businesses are, using Square's payroll system is probably a great idea, because it can sync up all of your data together, including sales and hours.

While I have never personally used Square in any aspect of my business, numerous of my business friends have and really love it. I've heard excellent things about their phone app as well, and you can actually run your payroll from your mobile device, which is pretty useful if you're often on the go.

You can run payroll through an in-house system, but if you have a small amount of employees it's really, honestly not worth the hassle.

PROPER PRICING: HOW TO MAKE MONEY

A lot of new businesses struggle with pricing. It's tempting to undercut your competition at all costs, but you end up either barely scraping by or outright losing money in the long run. Those who think they can make so much by upcharging, too, end up losing in the long run.

Finding that balance, and saving money where you can, is important. Let's talk about best pricing practices, and how to make your dollar go father when you are spending it.

HOW TO PRICE YOUR GOODS

If you never went to business school, you probably never learned how to properly price products. That's totally okay, I'm absolutely not here to judge your background. We all learn somewhere.

Pricing is complicated, so I'm going to try and break it down as much as I can. Please note that I cannot tell you how much to sell your baked goods for – that's completely on you, as a business owner. You control the prices. I can give you a guideline on how to figure out a price that is fair for you and for your customers.

RAW MATERIALS COST

First, it's important to figure out your raw materials cost for a batch of, well, anything. Sugar cookies are cheaper to make than muffins, which are cheaper than macarons. You need to do this calculation for every single item you make. However, once you lay the groundwork, it gets a lot easier. All of the numbers I'm going to offer you are examples, not set in stone. You're going to need to do the math for your own prices.

Let's say, for example, you're spending $30 on 50 pounds of flour. There's about 4 cups of flour in a pound, so we know that 50 pound bag has approximately 200 cups of flour, when measured perfectly, so 0.15 cents per cup. At $20 for 50 pounds of sugar, with 2 cups per pound, you have about 100 cups of sugar per 50 pound bag, costing you about 0.20 cents per cup. (Generally I get a little over two cups per pound, but we're going to round down here).

Baking soda is $12 per 15 pounds, and there are... a lot, of teaspoons in a pound. A lot. It's about 1,400 teaspoons in there, or 480 tablespoons, so we're going to say .03 cents per tablespoon. I can get 55 pounds of good quality butter for $130, arguably my biggest expense here, which works out to be about $1.60/pound. A gallon of decent vanilla extract sets me back about $200, but again, a gallon lasts a long time. At 768 teaspoons, or 256 tablespoons, it's about 0.79 cents per tablespoon.

I buy my eggs by the case, with 15 dozen in each case at $30/case. That is 180 eggs per case, or about 0.17 cents per egg.

Let's say this is a recipe I'm making in my shop. Again,

amounts of just examples, please don't make this recipe...
it not real.

5 cups flour

1 tablespoon baking soda

1 pound butter

3 cups sugar

2 eggs

1 tablespoon vanilla extract

This recipe makes, lets say, 100 cookies.

The flour, at $0.15/cup, costs $0.75.

The baking soda, at $0.03/tablespoon, costs $0.03.

The butter, at $1.50/pound, costs $1.50.

The sugar, at $0.20/cup, costs $0.60.

The eggs, at $0.17/egg, costs $0.34.

The vanilla, at $0.79/tablespoon, costs $0.79.

In total, these 100 cookies cost $4.18, or under $0.05/cookie. That price is your raw materials cost for this single item. You can work this out for each and every recipe you have to determine a good 'base' cost that each and every item you sell costs you to produce. When you have a chance in price or a change in suppliers, you should change your calculations to determine how much that changes your raw materials cost.

OTHER EXPENSES TO CONSIDER, TOO

But you can't just price your items at the raw materials expenses. You're going to lose a ton of money, because you have so many more expenses.

First to consider is your own time. If it takes you an hour to make these cookies, pay yourself – or your employee, but we'll get into employees soon – a fair wage. At $20/hour, you're adding at least another $0.20 per cookie, bringing our cookie cost to a minimum of $0.25.

Then let's think about the electricity you used to make that cookie, and just to keep the lights on. The water, to wash all of your dishes. The packaging for that cookie.

You need to work your pricing so that you're not just covering the obvious costs of the cookie, like the flour and the sugar, but the other costs as well. You should be able to at least keep the lights on!

CONSIDER WHAT OTHERS ARE PRICING

While you should never price your goods at a certain point 'just because' someone else is selling theirs at another specific price, you can get a good idea of what the competition is paying by looking at the price of their goods.

Check out a comparable bakery in your area, or in the surrounding area. You should have already done this when you were conducting research, so you shouldn't have any trouble pulling this information up. What are they charging for their sugar cookies, or their muffins, or whatever overlapping product you have? You may have to go online and do some research, especially if you're an online-only bakery, or working out of a small town with no comparable bakery.

However, this should help you see if your prices are outrageous, in which case you need to figure out how to fix that, or if you're potentially not charging enough, undercutting yourself.

CALCULATE YOUR OPERATING COSTS

The operating costs are exactly what I mentioned above – the costs to keep the doors open and the lights on. How much each month does your electric run? What about water? Sewage, etc? If you're not sure about these numbers, talk to your landlord if you're renting a space. They should be able to provide you with helpful information from their own experience or from previous tenants.

If you're selling, let's say 500 of those $0.25/cookie sugar cookies a month, and your overhead costs are an additional $1,000 to keep the lights on, you need 'tack' that price onto the cookie price. That's an extra $2/cookie, or at minimum $2.25/cookie just to break even. At that point, anything else you add onto that price is profit for your business.

That profit is very important, so let's talk about that, too.

You really never want to cut your money so close that you're barely scraping by. Most new businesses aren't profitable in their first months, and sometimes even years, so I'm not saying you should be rolling in the green, Scrooge McDuck-style, but you need to make sure you have some breathing room in case something happens.

In the first year of operating my bakery, I had a catastrophe. I had purchased my mixer second hand at an auction a few towns over. It was a big old Hobart commercial mixer that everyone – and I mean everyone – promised me would outlive me and my bakery. It came from an Italian restaurant that had shut down, and I got it for a song.

The reason I got it for a song was that it needed serious work, but I had no idea. This isn't a lesson on doing research before buying, but it is a lesson on having an emergency business fund. Without financial padding, my business would have died before it ever really even came to be. I ended up having to have to have a professional come out and service my machine, and replace some expensive parts.

That Hobart, by the way, is still going strong – though it's needed some additional work in the years since. The wiggle room I had worked into my pricing meant I wasn't just barely scraping by, and I was able to cover this (and other) unexpected expenses.

SAVING MONEY: BE SMART

A friend told me this story a long time ago, and it's going to stick with me for a while. I'm going to share it with you, so you can also learn from this woman's mistake.

When my friend was young, her first real boyfriend's mother owned a bar. The ideal teenage hookup, right? Well, my friend ended up offering to help in the back a few times a week cooking after they had a few people leave back to back. This was absolutely a mistake, and the woman was crazy, but that's not what this story is about.

My friend discovered the owner, her boyfriend's mother, bought their supplies from the grocery store. Ground beef? Grocery store, in those 3 pound packages. Burger buns? Local grocery store. Even the ketchup came in the standard size squeeze bottles you can buy on the supermarket shelf.

This is not the way you run your business, friend. I can't imagine their food costs, and when I inquired about the woman's business experience, my friend said she had zero, and the bar changed ownership not long after my friend had broken up with the boy.

No surprise. I cannot begin to imagine that woman's food costs.

Restaurants and bakeries really don't buy from the local store, for a number of reasons. Usually, your bakery is open when those stores are open, so you don't have the chance. Besides, they sell in a quantity for an average home or family. I use pounds and pounds of flour, butter, and sugar each and every day in my bakery. I would spend as much time opening those tiny 5 pound bags as I would actually baking with them, if that was the route I thought we should take.

Instead, I buy in bulk. I now work with a supplier who delivers our bulk goods once a week, but when I first started out, I shopped at the local restaurant supply store. I'm sure you have one within a relatively reasonable driving distance.

Most of the time, these stores are not open to the public, but here's some good news… once you register your business, you're not "the public". You're a bakery, a business, and you have access.

Depending on the store near you, you may need to register your name and business with them. If you live in a larger city, you may have multiple restaurant supply stores in your area. Shop around to find who has your 'bakery staples' the cheapest.

Flour, butter, and all types of sugar can be bought at these stores for fractions of the prices you'd find at your local store. It blows my mind when I talk to new business owners about their expenses just to find they're buying name brand butter in the 4 stick wrappers just down the street.

Buy in as large of quantities as you can reasonably, safely store. Restaurant supply stores have large bins for keeping dry goods fresh and ready to use, so I highly recommend you investing in those you can buy large quantities of the basics. If you have a storefront and a commercial kitchen available to you at all times, you should be able to figure out fairly quickly where things should belong and how much space you have for bulk buying. If you're working from your home kitchen, or traveling to a shared kitchen, it becomes a little harder – but the savings is worth the strategic thinking, without a doubt.

If you for some reason don't have a restaurant supply store that sells the bulk goods you need in your area, you may have to get creative. Your first step should be the bulk foods store, and talking with the owner. Not far from where I grew up was a Mennonite community, and there was a bulk foods store run by their community. I could buy 'bags' of seasonings, flour, and more. Talking with the owner one day, I found out you could also purchase full 50 pound bags of these things from them directly at a discount.

Finally, if you're absolutely sure you have exhausted all other options, consider ordering online. Websites like WebstaurantStore and others cater to small and medium sized restaurants or bakeries that don't have local access to supply chains, and ship. For $25, for example, you can get a 50 pound bag of name brand hi-gluten flour. That is still significantly cheaper than what you would pick up at a regular store near you.

Avoid Waste

This sounds obvious, but I can't tell you how many new bakers think they'll just "make extra", just in case. Making the appropriate amount of goods for any given day is hard, even for experienced bakery owners, and there's no worse feeling than running out or turning away a paying customer. However, tossing a huge amount of product at the end of the day isn't just wasteful, it's money that you're literally throwing in the garbage.

If you're an online-only bakery or a catering bakery, you should be making your baked goods to order. Seems obvious? It's not to everyone, so it bears repeating. You should never just be sitting on a stockpile of items just in case someone decides to order your goods. Making things fresh won't just ensure your customers get the best items possible – it also helps prevent waste.

If you're in a more traditional bakery, figuring out exactly how much to make gets a little more tricky. You're going to need to look at past sales for similar days (last Tuesday's sales, for example, will help you determine how much to make this Tuesday), and if there are any events happening. If there is something going on downtown this week, and your bakery is downtown, you're probably going to see an increase in traffic, so you should make more of your most popular items.

In order to best avoid waste, you need to keep detailed logs. This is something most new bakers don't think about, but if you don't keep a log of what you made and what you sold, you're never going to be able to accurately determine what you need to make.

Each morning when you're prepping and baking for the day, record how many of what items you made. 200 sugar cookies? Write it down. 10 muffins of each type, five types? Write it down. When you're first starting, a simple Excel or Google Sheet that you just plug in numbers for each day is all you really need.

At the end of the day, record your waste. Sell all of your apple cinnamon muffins, but have 5 chocolate chip left over? Mark it. Tomorrow, or next week, when you go to make your goods for the morning, you know that apple cinnamon sells better than chocolate chip, so you can adjust production as needed.

You're never going to get that perfect zero, where you sell everything but everyone has exactly what they want. However, you can get close enough that you're not throwing away 100s of dollars of goods each day, and saving yourself both money and hassle.

OTHER TIPS TO KEEP COSTS LOW

Ultimately, your situation is going to be unique. Your business will be at least a little different from any other business, so you need to keep a look out where you specifically can save money. However, I can provide some easy, practical tips that apply to a broad range of bakeries.

Do what you can yourself, at least at first. This is huge! It's tempting to hire help immediately, to outsource everything you can, and offload some work onto others. I'm not saying you're lazy, but it can be a lot, and getting help makes it feel more manageable. However, you're paying for that help, too.

You always need to balance paying for help with being able to afford that help. If it's something that you can do yourself, properly, and you have the time to do it, do it.

The first few years of opening a business is a lot of work. A lot, a lot. You're going to be dedicating hours and hours of time to your business, outside of normal business hours, and end up with a lot of late nights.

What you put into your business, you're going to get out of your business. The blood, sweat, and tears you put into it will come back to you, and the time you're willing to dedicate to working hard and focusing on making your business a success will be worth it.

When buying equipment, consider going used. I know I just told you my Hobart Horror Story, but honestly? Even with the expensive surprise bill, that Hobart has paid for itself time and time again. The sad reality is that many small restaurants and businesses fail. Twenty percent fail within their first year, 30% in the second year, and a staggering 50% fail within 5 years. That leaves a lot of product unused.

If you're buying bakery equipment for your location, or even your home, check out auctions and used marketplaces. You can score restaurant quality equipment significantly cheaper than you would be able to buy it used. It's a really great way to keep your money going farther, and keep you financially on the right track. No matter where you're located in the US, there's a good chance there is an auction company near you that handles major resale of goods.

CONSIDER SEASONAL SPECIALTIES

When things are in season, they're cheaper. As a consumer, you're probably already aware of that. Summer berries aren't just the cheapest way to buy them, but they are also the best berries. In fall, everything pumpkin is cheaper.

Buying, baking with, and selling seasonal goods makes sense. They are significantly cheaper in season than out of season, and you'll save a bunch of money. It's also fun to highlight the seasons in your baking, at least in my opinion, and consumers enjoy this sort of thing. It's a win-win all around.

CONSIDER GROWING OR PRODUCING YOUR OWN

This is not an option for everyone, but I have a friend who grows her own mint for her baked goods. She has a lovely little collection of herbs in a store room with a grow lamp, and it costs her almost nothing to keep them going.

My mother in law also raises chickens. I've never professionally baked with her eggs, but for my personal use, they're fantastic. If you have a smaller scale bakery, you could absolutely have your own chickens for eggs, or grow your own produce and herbs.

It's not just raw materials like this, either. Did you know powdered sugar, sometimes called confectioners' sugar or icing sugar, is approximately 200% more expensive than regular granulated sugar? I use a ton of powered sugar in my bakery each day, and that cost was adding up. I bought a powerful, industrial blender – an upfront purchase, of course – and blitz my much cheaper granulated sugar, creating powered sugar.

My favorite money saving tip I have is to make my own yogurt or buttermilk for recipes. It's not hard to culture these, and it actually does save quite a bit of money in the long run. I love baking with buttermilk for a rich, tangy addition, too.

Waste Not, Want Not

You've heard this phrase, right? I grew up with that.

Well, that, and "beggars can't be choosers". My grandmother, and to an extent my mother, was raised in a very different time. You didn't just throw something away, you found a way to repurpose and reuse it. You couldn't waste food, and even if that bread was a little stale, well, you'd better figure it out.

Instead of wasting and tossing leftovers, find a way to repurpose it. Figure out what you end up 'wasting', and be sure to repurpose it. Leftover bread can be croutons, sweeter options can be a French toast bake or a bread pudding... be smart about it, and you can prevent most of your 'waste' from ever seeing the inside of a trash cash.

CONTINUING TO GROW

As a business, evolving, changing, and growing is a big part of, well, being a successful business. If you're not adapting and changing, you're going to end up behind the curve.

In that regard, you should always consider how to continue to grow and expand, but in a sustainable way. What does sustainable business growth mean, and what does it look like? Let's talk about that – and some easy, painless ways you can grow your business without stressing yourself out.

Too often, I see a successful business end up flat on their face, deeply in debt or struggling to survive. If they're successful, why are they flailing, you might ask?

It's because they tried to expand too quickly, or do too much, and put themselves so far behind no recovery is possible.

Most small businesses that have this problem have never heard of the term SGR, or Sustainable Growth Rate. This is a business term, but it basically represents the max amount of growth or expansion that a business can sustain without putting themselves under serious financial strain, or major debt. Make sense?

Think of a floor to ceiling situation. The floor is the absolute minimum in sales you need to make to stay afloat and in business. The ceiling is the maximum in sales you can achieve without putting yourself under financial strain, like emptying your business savings or getting new financing.

Alright, in a less technical way, you should never grow

your business at the expense of, well, your business. You should never choose growth if it means acquiring more debt than the company can handle, or sacrificing quality or service. This doesn't mean that your growth has to be extremely slow, it just means that you need to be smart about it.

There are a few things you can do, and elements you can incorporate into your business, to ensure sustainable growth.

Customer satisfaction is the biggest one, in my opinion. I have said this at least a half dozen times in this book, but it bears repeating as we near the end. The happier your customers are, the more likely they are to return – and bring friends. Maintaining a happy customer base will grow your business in ways you can't imagine.

Always making choices that cater to the customer will help you continue to grow, and feed into your customer satisfaction. You want to do a line of high end cookies with exotic flavors? That's awesome, and I'm excited for you – unless your customers are not interested in lavender and rosemary, cardamom and rosewater. Then, you're probably just wasting your time and resources to only make yourself happy. Your decisions to change and grow should always be rooted in your customers needs.

I touched on this topic when writing a business plan, but having clear, achievable goals (preferably using the SMART system) is the best, and frankly the only, way that you can continue to grow. If you don't have goals and you're just sort of feeling around in the dark, hoping for the best, you're going to have a rough time. Goals isn't a business buzz-word type of situation, and sometimes you might feel like you're wasting time writing them, but they really make the difference in the long run.

Being open to new ideas, feedback, and even help is also absolutely huge, especially when you're just starting out. It's so easy for new business owners to be defensive or unable to see their business from anyone else's perspective, but if you can step out of yourself and your ego for a second, you may be able to really come at a problem with a new solution and do something great. If you are never open to trying something new or changing something, nothing will ever change. That's a fact.

How Do I Even Get New Ideas?!

I get it! Figuring out new product lines, concepts, and what your customer really wants can be overwhelming. At a certain point, you might be so bogged down with the day to day workings of your business that you can barely surface to get a breath of fresh air, let alone another new idea.

I'm going to encourage you to not live this way, overwhelmed with work, for long, but even if you are (and maybe you like it! Some folks thrive on it), you need to keep thinking ahead.

Asking your customers what they want is going to be the best way that you can figure out the direction you need to take. Seriously, ask!

You could send an email out to your email list that asks them to fill out a short survey of what they want to see in your bakery case next. A Twitter poll, or even just a Facebook post asking what your customers want can go a long way. If you have regulars that are your ideal target market, as them what they would like to see from your bakery next. These people are the ones keeping your business afloat, so keep an open mind.

THOUGHTS ON EXPANSION

My best expansion idea for my own bakery was getting an espresso machine. Did you know those things are crazy expensive?! I had to shell out a ton of cash for the machine, and then an experienced barista to run it and teach everyone else. I partnered with a local coffee roaster to carry their beans, and while they were more expensive than what my bulk supplier could get me, my customers valued local and small.

I crafted the ideas for drinks based around what I had in the bakery case, working on the same concept as wine tasting – this blueberry muffin is complimented by this honey vanilla latte.

It ended up paying off, and I sell more espresso than drip coffee now. I knew my customers liked local products, and espresso. I knew that given the chance, I could craft a killer coffee menu, having basically lived on the stuff the first few years my business was around and growing. And I was able to source not only the products – the beans, the machine – but the talent, like a barista who could explain to me the difference between under versus over extracted shots and why timing your pull matters.

Maybe coffee isn't where you want to go, though. Expanding into the breakfast and lunch market, though, could open you up to more people through the door, and especially during your slower points. You may be able to bake many of the parts you need, and adding on some simple choices – sandwiches, wraps, and soups, for example – could be fairly easy, with a low equipment investment.

As always, I'm going to take this time to push seasonal lines and expansions, too. Everyone loves living within the season, and in my experience, you cannot go wrong with using fresh, local produce or ingredients when expanding your products. Pumpkin in the fall, strawberries in the summer, squash in the late summer and early fall... be sure to let your customers know it's in season and picked at peak freshness.

EXPANDING YOUR TEAM

At a certain point you may be limited not by the sales coming in, but your ability to produce them. At this point, you're going to need to expand your team, so revisit my section on hiring and training new employees.

The decision to expand your team shouldn't be taken lightly. Someone is trusting you with their livelihood, and you'll need to be sure that you can afford to pay them a fair wage and have enough work for them.

Expanding your team isn't just a good idea when looking to grow your business, though. If you're run thin and feeling overwhelmed, even hiring someone for a few hours a week can make a big difference in giving you a moment to step back, breathe, and reexamine what you're doing and how to take it to the next level.

I'll admit this to you now, at the end of the book – I had a really, really hard time at first letting go and hiring someone else. I wanted to touch it all, do it all, be involved at every single step. My business was and still is my baby, and it was so important to me to ensure it ran properly.

I worried that if I let go, if I put someone else in charge of anything, it would all fall apart.

Spoiler alert: it would have fallen apart if I hadn't relinquished control, because there was no way I could have ever expanded and grown just by myself. I needed a team around me, and at some point you will, too.

Don't be afraid to hire someone to help take something off your plate, so you can handle other things. Or really, just so you can feel human again for a few hours, instead of constantly feeling stressed or anxious about your business.

OPENING BRICK AND MORTAR FOR EXPANSION

If you're an online-only business, your first step into expansion may just be a real location. Whether you choose a more traditional bakery or a takeout-only option is up to you, but you don't actually have to go any farther than this book.

I've included plenty of information about finding the right location, doing market research, and more. There is a lot in here that can help you make the right choice when the time comes to expand outward and upward.

There are a few extra things you need to pay special attention to when you're making this decision. For one, is your clientele going to follow you? I would recommend you continue an online storefront and presence, especially fi you have customers who are far enough away from your hometown that they would never be able to stop in and pick up their orders.

Be sure you can accommodate everyone, both your current online customers and any new customers you're going to bring in with your store. It's not a one or the other thing, it's a do both sort of thing. If you can't juggle them both, that is completely okay, but don't try and let down both sets of customers.

Make sure your target market matches up with your new location – or, consider what market you can fit into your current branding and products. Your target market in a physical location may be different from who you are used to targeting online, and that is completely okay! As long as they are interested in what you have to sell, they are part of your market.

Finally, be realistic. I've said this a few times in this book, but it bears repeating. Opening a brick and mortar location is a huge undertaking, and it can be a lot to deal with. Make sure that you have plenty of support and help so that you can maintain your current business while opening the location.

OPENING A SECOND LOCATION

This can be a big risk, but opening a new location can also open up a whole lot of opportunities for you and your business. Deciding if it's right for you, though, is a big step.

Can you afford to open another location? Is the money that you're making from your current location enough to help float the business until it becomes profitable – and you should have an idea of how long that will be, because you went through it with your first. Look at the sales data from your first year. When did you start making money? You can expect at least that long with your second location.

How much funding will you need to open your second location? It's not exactly cheap to open a bakery, which you obviously know, since you've done it once before. Depending on where you're going to end up, location wise, you may be spending more or less money setting up your new shop, getting the kitchen ready, etc.

How will you get this funding? Are you taking out a bank loan? Are you getting an investor? Are you pulling mostly from your savings, or doing some combination? Take time to really consider the benefits, and consequences, of adding on debt to the company or pulling from an emergency fund.

Choosing a second location can also be tricky. You need to ensure that you are far enough away from your current location that you aren't directly competing with yourself, but your target market still shops in these places. However, put them too far away from each other, and going back and forth to each location can end up a huge hassle.

Finally, be absolutely sure you have a team around you that you trust. You physically cannot be in two places at once – it just doesn't work. I have my niece and her husband running my first, and largest, location, and an employee who has been with me for years, since the start, running my second location. Without a team of people looking out for the business, I could not have even thought about opening a second location.

Conclusion

You've made it to the end. Congratulations! I hope you've found some help and inspiration in this book.

As I mentioned previously, this isn't really a one-and-done type of read. Instead, as you continue to grow, expand, or even start your journey, you may need to visit different chapters or sections to help motivate you or give you ideas. That's exactly the way I wrote it, and I hope this book continues to be a source of help and inspiration in your journey forward.

I'm going to leave you with some parting advice, if you don't mind. Just a tidbit or two that didn't fit anywhere else, but is Important for you to keep in mind moving forward.

Burnout is Real: Be Wary

I'm not going to get on a soap box and preach to you for 5 pages about the "hustle culture" that the internet has cultivated in the last few years. The idea of this is that you always want to be pushing, be working, be striving for something better.

Theoretically, that is great, and actually true. You always want to be moving forward, where ever that forward is, and building a better future for yourself. I can get behind that.

In practice, though, it's important to remember that we're all just human. We're not robots, we can't work 13 hour days 7 days a week with no break, at least not for very long. You're not just going to feel awful and exhausted and run down, but you're going to end up being less effective overall.

Building a business from the ground up doesn't leave a lot of time for a healthy work life balance, or self care, and there are going to be days that are hard. It will be difficult to find the motivation to get out of bed, let alone get dressed and handle what you need to. I won't lie to you there – It Is hard, especially at first.

Make sure you're taking care of yourself to avoid burnout. If you need to pause and step away from production for ten minutes to look at funny pictures online or call your best friend, do it! If you need to hire someone else for 10 hours a week to wash dishes and package goods so you don't have to, do it (as long as it fits in your financial budgets, of course).

It's so hard to find a good balance, but keep striving for one. You deserve it.

It's Not Always Easy

There's a reason that not everyone has started a business, and not every business that is started succeeds. It's not always going to be easy, and in the early dreaming stages, you may not realize that. It's easy to gloss over the hard parts and focus on the fun parts, like spending your days decorating cakes and cookies or developing recipes that people will love.

It is, however, worth it.

The most rewarding thing I've ever done in my life is abandon my career and jump into the bakery business. I'm thankful every single day that I had the support and love of my family, and was able to make these decisions.

It was hard. The sleepless nights, worrying about if something was going to work out. The early mornings, prepping for events or just for open. The stress of hiring people, of firing people, of balancing checkbooks and learning about taxes. I ate more fast food late at night in the first few years, drank more cheap coffee, and had far too much raw egg in the form of batter than is ever healthy for a single person to consume. It almost broke my marriage, because even though my partner was loving and supportive I didn't know how to ask for help, didn't know how to let go, and I really struggled.

It was so worth it.

Pause when you need to, step away when you have to, and take care of yourself. But don't stop fighting for your dreams, even when it gets hard, because you're so much stronger than you know – and you can make this business a success. If you dream it, you believe in it, and you work hard, you can really get where you want to be.

I did it. Now it's your turn.

Thank You!

Would you please consider writing a review where you purchased this book online? Thanks!

Made in the USA
Las Vegas, NV
15 January 2024

84440356R00144